CULTURES OF THE WORLD
Nicaragua

Cavendish Square

New York

Published in 2016 by Cavendish Square Publishing, LLC
243 5th Avenue, Suite 136, New York, NY 10016
Copyright © 2016 by Cavendish Square Publishing, LLC

Third Edition

CPSIA Compliance Information: Batch #CW16CSQ

All websites were available and accurate when this book was sent to press.

Cataloging-in-Publication Data

Kott, Jennifer.
Nicaragua / by Jennifer Kott, Kristi Streiffert, and Debbie Nevins.
p. cm. — (Cultures of the world)
Includes index.
ISBN 978-1-5026-0806-2 (hardcover) ISBN 978-1-5026-0807-9 (ebook)
1. Nicaragua — Juvenile literature. I. Kott, Jennifer, 1971-. II. Streiffert, Kristi. III. Nevins, Debbie. IV. Title.
F1523.2 K66
972.85—d23

Writers, Jennifer Kott, Kristi Streiffert; Debbie Nevins, third edition
Editorial Director, third edition: David McNamara
Editor, third edition: Debbie Nevins
Art Director, third edition: Jeffrey Talbot
Designer, third edition: Jessica Nevins
Senior Production Manager, third edition: Jennifer Ryder-Talbot
Cover Picture Researcher: Stephanie Flecha
Picture Researcher, third edition: Jessica Nevins

PRECEDING PAGE
Dancers at a festival twirl in traditional dress.

Printed in the United States of America

CONTENTS

NICARAGUA TODAY

NICARAGUA IS THE "LAND OF LAKES AND VOLCANOES." FIFTY volcanoes—seven of them still active—dominate the scenery, often reflecting in the lake waters at their feet. In Lake Nicaragua, the country's largest lake, the island of Ometepe is the world's largest volcanic island inside a freshwater lake. The island was created by the Concepción and Maderas volcanoes. Unlike its partner, Concepción is still active and therefore still growing.

Nicaragua is also the "land of poets" where "everyone is a poet until proved otherwise." It's home to the city of Granada, "the Paris of Central America." These delightful appellations hint at a place of rare beauty and culture. Indeed, Nicaragua is also a land of lush tropical rain forests and cloud forests; white sand beaches with swaying palms on the Caribbean Sea; rivers and lagoons; and colorful, old Spanish cities.

For birdlovers, this Central American country is a paradise. Its seven hundred species include birds of exquisite and sometimes iridescent hues, such as the turquoise-browed motmot. Nicaraguans call it the *guardabaranco*, or "ravine guard," and have designated it as the national bird. This green, blue, black, and rust

The guardabaranco is Nicaragua's national bird.

beauty lives in the western forests. The resplendent quetzal, a bird so beautiful its very name means "magnificent plumage," resides in the cloud forests. The waters surrounding the Solentiname Islands of Lake Nicaragua turn pink with wading crowds of elegant roseate spoonbills.

For these reasons and many others, some predict Nicaragua will be "the next Costa Rica." By that they mean Nicaragua is poised to be the next "hot" tourist destination, the place to see before it's "discovered," when rampant tourism, along with increasing numbers of commercial businesses, will destroy its untouched splendor.

This paradise has another face, however, and it's not pretty. Nicaragua has been marred by an ugly history. Tyranny, poverty, foreign intervention, corruption, political violence, wars, and natural disasters have cost Nicaragua a great deal and its people have suffered much. However, recent years have slowly brought a time of relative stability and peace, helping the nation emerge from its long trauma.

Living conditions have improved for many Nicaraguans as clean water and sanitation have become more available. In 2010, about 85 percent of the population had access to an improved water source. About 52 percent had access to improved sanitation facilities. (The World Health Organization/ UNICEF Joint Monitoring Programme for Water Supply and Sanitation has specific definitions for "improved" sources and facilities.) These figures represent a significant improvement, though they are far from ideal. Rural areas, in particular, have much less access to clean water and sanitation— making the people who live in those areas far more susceptible to disease.

Overall, however, life expectancy in Nicaragua has increased from 53.7 years in 1970 to 74.5 years in 2012. Literacy has also increased significantly, largely as a result of the Sandinistas' Literacy Crusade. This project, one of the

first things the Sandinistas embarked upon following the revolution, earned the prestigious UNESCO Literacy Award in 1980. Other literacy campaigns followed and resulted in a population that is mostly literate, as opposed to not, which had been the case under the Somoza dictatorship. As of 2015, the literacy rate stood at about 83 percent. This figure also reflects the fact that more children are attending school and are staying in school longer. Again, however, the urban figures tend to exceed the rural ones.

Economic indicators are also improving, for the most part. The economy grew 4.7 percent in 2014, despite a steep decline in coffee revenues due to a fungus that year—and coffee is the country's leading export. Nevertheless, the fact remains that Nicaragua is the second poorest country in the Americas after Haiti. Even President Daniel Ortega admits his administration has been unable to budge that unfortunate statistic.

Poverty hampers a country's efforts to improve all other sectors of society, including, of course, its efforts to reduce poverty. No doubt that is a leading

Residents of a poor neighborhood in Tipitapa, some 15.5 miles (25 km) from Managua, live in homes of corrugated metal, plywood, and any other materials the people can find.

A man in Juigalpa sprays graffiti on a mural of President Daniel Ortega during a protest against the construction of the canal.

reason why Ortega is collaborating with a Chinese billionaire who wants to build the Grand Trans-oceanic Nicaraguan Canal. This massive engineering project, if built, will provide a water route through the country from the Atlantic coast to the Pacific. The canal will offer marine traffic an alternative to the Panama Canal, and will presumably make lots of money for its investor and also for Nicaragua. Ortega announced that the undertaking will bring thousands of jobs to the country. For starters, however, the project has definitely brought an enormous amount of controversy, mainly from alarmed environmentalists. Indigenous people who stand to be pushed off their lands are also in opposition.

The canal could easily be said to be Nicaragua's greatest controversy today, along with, some could argue, Daniel Ortega himself. He remains a popular president. He won the 2011 election by a much greater margin than he did the 2007 election. Some accuse Ortega of softening in his older years, giving up some of his former socialist stances. If so, it hasn't necessarily had the result of making him into a more flexible, adaptable leader. Critics say Ortega is embracing whatever it takes to stay in power.

It does seem possible that Ortega, his wife, and family are becoming a political dynasty—the very thing he so despised years ago. In 2014, Nicaragua's National Assembly—with a majority being FSLN, Ortega's own party—approved changes to the nation's constitution that eliminate presidential term limits. This will not only allow Ortega to run for a third successive term in 2016 but for more terms after that—for the rest of his life if he wishes. Some critics see Ortega's wife Rosario Murillo behind the power-grabbing machinations. The energetic first lady is the official voice of the government and appears in public far more often than her

husband. More and more, she seems to be the gatekeeper for access to her husband. She is also a Cabinet minister overseeing social issues and programs, and some observers suspect she may well be looking to run for president herself.

Murillo, a poet and an artist, has certainly left her mark on Nicaraguan society. In 2013, using state monies, she dressed the nation's capital in fanciful, brightly colored "Tree of Life" statues—40-foot-tall (12-meters-tall) metal trees with curlicue branches. About fifty of them were installed at traffic intersections throughout Managua, and there are reportedly plans for a hundred more. She has also erected several other huge art installations and monuments, all with nationalistic themes.

Meanwhile, Ortega has allegedly made himself and his family immensely rich through multi-million-dollar business ventures, which strikes certain leftists as quite objectionable.

Is the Daniel Ortega presidency going sour? Time will tell. Some critics have already reached their conclusions. "It was a beautiful revolution," said the leftist Nicaraguan poet Ernesto Cardenal in 2015. "But what happened is that it was betrayed. There is now the family dictatorship of Daniel Ortega. That's not what we fought for."

One of Rosario Murilla's "Tree of Life" installations can be seen next to a silhouetted statue of Augusto Sandino in Managua.

GEOGRAPHY

BELIZE

GUATEMALA

HONDURAS

EL SALVADOR

NICARAGUA

PACIFIC
OCEAN

COSTA
RICA

Nicaragua is the largest country in Central America.

NICARAGUA IS A LAND IN BETWEEN. It sits on a strip of land between two great oceans—the Atlantic and the Pacific—and it has coastlines on both. It also sits on the land that links two great continents—North America and South America. Nicaragua is the largest of the seven countries on the Central American isthmus, or land bridge, along with Belize, Guatemala, Honduras, El Salvador, Costa Rica, and Panama. This region is part of the North American continent but is called Central America.

To the north of Nicaragua lies Honduras, and to the south is Costa Rica. The western border is the Pacific Ocean, and to the east is the Caribbean Sea, which joins the Atlantic Ocean. In all, Nicaragua has about 560 miles (900 kilometers) of coastline. At 49,998 square miles (129,494 square kilometers), Nicaragua is a little smaller than Louisiana. Large areas of the country are uninhabited; most of its people are concentrated in the western region and in a few cities. The country's population per square mile is relatively low compared to other Central American countries.

1

Nicaragua's Cerro Negro ("Black Hill") volcano is the youngest volcano in Central America. It first appeared in 1850. Since its birth, it has erupted at least twenty-three times (as of 2015), most recently in 1999.

THREE REGIONS

Nicaragua is divided into three geographic regions: the western Pacific lowlands, the central highlands, and the eastern Caribbean lowlands (also called the Mosquito Coast). Each region has features and weather characteristics that differentiate it from other parts of the country.

PACIFIC LOWLANDS Three out of four Nicaraguans live in the western part of the country between the Pacific Coast and Lake Managua. Here, the land is good for crop cultivation because it has been enriched over the years by volcanic ash. Many of the people who live here work on farms, but Nicaragua's three biggest cities, León, Managua, and Granada, are also in this region. The largest is Managua, the nation's capital.

CENTRAL HIGHLANDS East of Managua lies the area known as the central highlands. This mountainous area is covered with dense rain forest and receives an annual rainfall of between 70 and 100 inches (1,800 and 2,540 millimeters).

This is an inspiring, beautiful land of coffee plantations and cool, misty forests. In the northern mountains is a rich mining district called Nueva Segovia. Few people are willing to live in this humid place and take up the difficult work of mining the area's silver and gold.

MOSQUITO COAST Even wetter than the central highlands is the Mosquito Coast, which runs along the eastern third of the country. This region is the wettest area in Central America, with average annual rainfall ranging from 100 to 250 inches (2,540 to 6,350 mm). Much of the soil is gravel and sandy clay, with the only variation being a treeless, grassy plain called a savannah.

This area was named after the Miskito people, who have lived here for centuries. When the Spanish name, *Costa Miskito*, was translated into English, it became Mosquito Coast, possibly because the area was infested with mosquitoes. In addition to the Miskito, the other main groups who live here are the Rama and Sumo, who are natives of Nicaragua—and the Garífuna, who were originally from Africa. These groups have lived in this swamp-like

San Miguelito's wetlands are on the eastern shore of Lake Nicaragua.

region for many generations. Many build their houses on stilts for protection from floods and snakes.

Few Nicaraguans travel between the Pacific Coast and the Mosquito Coast. Only a few roads link the two sides of the country, so travel is mostly by plane and boat.

LAKES AND RIVERS

A network of waterways throughout Nicaragua play an important role in the country's system of transportation, commerce, and daily life. For example, the best farmland is near the lakes, rivers, and seas. Rivers mark the boundaries between Nicaragua and its neighbors Honduras and Costa Rica. City residents often take advantage of a sunny weekend by driving to one of the many resorts on the shores of Lake Nicaragua.

Nicaragua has two large lakes: Lake Managua and Lake Nicaragua. The larger of the two is Lake Nicaragua, also called by its more historical name,

A man fishes with a net on the shore of Lake Nicaragua. The Concepción volcano dominates the horizon.

THE NICARAGUA CANAL—FORTUNE OR FOLLY?

The idea of a canal across Nicaragua is centuries old. In 2014, one hundred years after the opening of the Panama Canal, work began on the proposed—and controversial—Nicaragua Canal.

Chinese billionaire businessman Wang Jing worked out a deal with the Nicaragua government to build the $50 billion project. The inter-oceanic canal would offer an alternative to the Panama Canal, which cannot handle certain very large ships. Global maritime traffic is expected to increase in the coming years, which would cause further congestion in Panama. Supporters of the canal say a new route across the American continents is badly needed.

Canal opponents demonstrate in Managua in December 2014.

The government of President Daniel Ortega, meanwhile, says the project will benefit the country by providing some 250,000 jobs. The proposed route would make use of some of Nicaragua's rivers and lakes. In particular, it would cross Lake Nicaragua. This fact is one of several that environmentalists and other opponents have serious concerns about. The lake is a major source of drinking water and irrigation, and home to rare freshwater sharks. Opponents have many other objections as well, ranging from the ecological to the political to the economic. The financing, for example, seems shrouded in a fair amount of uncertainty. Also, with Nicaragua's volatile climate, active volcanoes, and numerous earthquakes, many people question if the canal is even possible.

Nevertheless, work proceeds. Wang Jing and Ortega have said that the project will be completed by 2019.

Lake Cocibolca. Measuring 45 miles (72.4 km) wide and 110 miles (177 km) long, it has three volcanoes and more than three hundred islands, most of which are inhabited. Lake Nicaragua is Central America's largest lake, and the world's nineteenth largest freshwater lake. Perhaps the most remarkable feature is its unique inhabitants—freshwater sharks. Río Tipitapa connects this lake to Lake Managua, which covers 390 square miles (1,010 square km).

The Río Coco Oregovia forms part of the border with Honduras, and the Río San Juan forms part of the border with Costa Rica before emptying into the Caribbean Sea. Other rivers important to Nicaragua's transportation system include the Escondido and the Río Grande.

Ever since Christopher Columbus sailed along the coast of what is now Nicaragua in the sixteenth century, explorers had hoped to find a passage that would connect the Pacific Ocean on the west to the Atlantic Ocean on the east. While the Río San Juan does run nearly from coast to coast, it is not suitable for heavy traffic by freighters and other large vessels.

In the nineteenth century, Americans and Europeans studied a plan to build a canal to join the two oceans, providing ships with a fast and inexpensive route between the east and west coasts of the United States. The US committee responsible for finding the best place to build the canal first chose Nicaragua, but disagreements with the Nicaraguan president resulted in Panama being selected as the site for the connecting waterway. The Panama Canal opened in 1914.

VOLCANOES AND OTHER NATURAL HAZARDS

Volcanoes are largely responsible for the geographic makeup of Nicaragua. Many lakes and islands were formed by volcanic activity. Cities developed near the volcanoes because fertile farmland there attracted early settlers.

At least a dozen active volcanoes and many more dormant ones give the landscape a beautiful quality, but these peaks also pose a threat to Nicaraguans. Most of the population lives near active volcanoes. Thus, at any time, their homes and crops could be destroyed by an eruption or an earthquake caused by underground volcanic activity. The city of Managua still bears the scars of one such devastating earthquake that occurred just

before Christmas in 1972. Managua is actually built on top of old volcanic rock that has been pressed together, not on solid rock.

Frequent earthquakes have caused destruction to Nicaragua throughout the country's history. The western part of the country lies along the Ring of Fire, a chain of volcanoes and fault lines that encircles the Pacific Ocean. It is called the Ring of Fire because of the high volume of volcanic activity there. Some of the volcanoes in Nicaragua that have erupted in the past two decades include Cerro Negro, Momotombo, San Cristóbal, Telica, and Concepción. Concepción and another volcano, Madera, make up Ometepe Island in Lake Nicaragua, on which at least eight small villages are built— proof that Nicaraguans have learned to coexist with the volcanoes that dominate the skyline.

Although living near the Ring of Fire can be dangerous, Nicaragua's turbulent government and economy have made it difficult to support research on volcanoes and earthquakes. Nevertheless, seismologists and volcanologists have set up stations in villages and cities located near

Concepción's colorful ash deposits and green slopes make for a beautiful sight on Ometepe Island.

volcanoes to monitor the earth's movements. The Nicaraguan Institute of Territorial Studies is also studying the volcanoes and their effects on the area.

Nicaragua's government is optimistic about using the country's abundant geothermal resources to reduce their need for imported oil. A geothermal plant near the Momotombo volcano, about 50 miles (80.5 km) from Managua, generates nonpolluting energy using the steam that rises from the depths of the volcano. There are plans to build more geothermal plants in Nicaragua in the near future.

Unfortunately, Nicaragua also suffers from other natural calamities that cause widespread destruction, such as drought, tsunamis, and hurricanes. Hurricane Mitch, which devastated Nicaragua and Honduras in October 1998, was one of the most deadly hurricanes to hit the Western Hemisphere in the modern era. The hurricane killed more than three thousand people and caused more than $1 billion in damages in Nicaragua, leaving thousands homeless and many of the country's roads destroyed.

CLIMATE AND SEASONS

Managua, the capital, is located about 87 degrees west of the prime meridian, at about the same longitude as Memphis, Tennessee, and lies about 12 degrees north of the equator. A line running east from Managua would pass about 1,025 miles (about 1,650 km) south of Miami.

As Nicaragua is located near the equator, it has a tropical climate—warm in the morning, hot and humid in the afternoon, and pleasant at night. In the mountainous regions of northwest Nicaragua, the higher altitude makes the average temperature a little cooler, especially at night. Also, the northern part of the country is a little less humid than the southern part. Even so, the weather in Nicaragua is hotter and more humid than what most North Americans are used to experiencing.

The climate in the eastern part of Nicaragua is always about the same—hot and wet. Few people live there because much of the land is covered with rain forest and jungle. It is the perfect home for monkeys, alligators, and snakes. Bananas, coconuts, persimmons, and other tropical fruit also thrive in this climate.

In the more densely populated western lowlands, there are two seasons: the wet season from May to November and the dry season from December to April. During the wet season, it rains heavily almost every day, and there is little warning before a storm. The hottest, driest months of the year are March and April. For a few weeks in July and August, the rain stops again, the weather gets very hot, and everyone suffers from the heat.

The average temperature in the lowlands is about 86 degrees Fahrenheit (30 degrees Celsius). The sun is blazing hot, and Nicaraguans often try to protect themselves from its damaging effects. Women sometimes carry umbrellas to provide some shade if they are out in the open for a long time. Men wear straw hats with strings that are tied into a knot under the chin to shade their eyes while working in the fields or walking outdoors.

Very few homes have air conditioning—in fact, most do not even have electric fans. In Managua, a few upper-class homes, offices, and restaurants have air conditioning, but most people just have to tolerate the heat. Despite the climate, over the years, young Nicaraguans faithfully followed fashion fads—even when it meant wearing *plásticos* (plast-EE-koh), or clothes made of plastic, a style that was popular in the discos in the mid-1980s.

A boy bikes through waters caused by the flooding of the Ochomogo River in October 2014.

MAJOR CITIES

MANAGUA With a population of about 2.2 million people, Managua is Nicaragua's largest city and its capital. Nearly one-fourth of the population lives here. From the top of *Loma de Tiscapa* ("Tiscapa Hill"), the whole city is visible. The most beautiful part of this view is the Tiscapa Lagoon, a shallow pond that shimmers in the sun. The lagoon, which formed after rainwater filled a crater made by a volcanic eruption, is surrounded by lush green trees.

The city has a drawback; since it is situated on a major fault line near a volcano, earthquakes occur frequently. An earthquake in December 1972 killed six thousand people and destroyed the city. Recovery has been a long, slow process that may never be completed. Parts of Managua still lie in ruins, and subsequent earthquakes have hindered plans to rebuild the city.

The government has decided not to rebuild anything in the worst-hit areas. Instead, new development in Managua—just as in many cities in the United States—has been outside the city where new neighborhoods, shops, and restaurants are being built.

Over the past decade, a few modern shopping malls with department stores and movie theaters have sprung up in Managua, along with numerous modern supermarkets and American fast food restaurants.

LEÓN AND GRANADA, both within 50 miles (80.5 km) of Managua, are very important to the history of Nicaragua, but they seem more like large towns than cities. León has about 201,000 people, and Granada, about 124,000. The two cities are regarded as sister cities. Neither have modern supermarkets or department stores similar to those found in Managua.

GRANADA Nicaragua's oldest city, Granada, was founded in 1524 by Spanish explorer Francisco Hernández de Córdoba. Like Managua, it is also located on the shore of a lake and near a volcano. It is the country's second-largest city and an important commercial area. Granada's volcano has left the area around the town fertile, and coffee and sugarcane are two important crops grown there.

Like all cities in Nicaragua, Granada has seen its share of fighting caused by political conflict, which has ravaged the country for years. Many factories and buildings have suffered heavy damage and are still being repaired. There are a hundred or so tiny islands east of Granada in Lake Nicaragua. These *isletas* (ees-LEH-tahs) are said to have been created when Granada's volcano erupted, blowing its lake-facing side into the water. The islands are linked by motorboat taxis, and wealthy Nicaraguans have built cottages there for weekend retreats.

LEÓN Hernández also founded León in 1524. The original site was about 20 miles (32 km) east of the present city, but it was abandoned in 1610 after a series of earthquakes. The ruins of the city, which were excavated in 1960, are called León Viejo. In 2000, UNESCO declared León Viejo a World Heritage Site.

In the Spanish colonial period, León was the capital of Nicaragua. It has a number of impressive cathedrals, including the Cathedral of León (built 1747—1814), the largest cathedral in Central America.

A colorful street in Granada looks toward the yellow Granada Cathedral.

NATURAL RESOURCES

Agriculture is an important part of life in Nicaragua. Almost half of the employed people work on farms. During the dry season, when crops are harvested, schools are closed so that children can help with the farm work.

Many crops—from beans and bananas to sugarcane and rice—grow well in Nicaraguan soil. Corn, coffee, cotton, tobacco, and cacao are the most important crops, while beans and rice are grown mainly for domestic consumption. The country's chief agricultural exports are coffee, beef, sugar, and seafood. Also important is gold. Other important minerals include silver, copper, tungsten, lead, and zinc.

Lake Nicaragua is the only freshwater lake in the world that is home to sharks. Stories of missing swimmers abound, but while people suspect the predatory inhabitants, no deaths have ever been documented as having been caused by shark attack.

The lake was probably formed long ago when volcanic activity cut the area off from the Pacific Ocean. For many years it was believed that marine life became trapped in the lake while it still contained salt water. As the character of the lake gradually changed to fresh water, the saltwater fish adapted to living in fresh water and were able to reproduce. Another theory is that sharks traveled back and forth between the Atlantic Ocean and the lake. In 1966, after a decade of research that involved putting identification tags on sharks, American zoologist Thomas B. Thorson reported that bull sharks, a ferocious and versatile predatory species, enter the lake via the Río San Juan from the Atlantic Ocean, looking for food. The sharks, which can grow to 10 feet (3 m) and weigh up to 400 pounds (181.4 kilograms), can adapt to fresh water.

Another typically saltwater species found in the lake is the sawfish, which can weigh up to 1,000 pounds (453.6 kg). In the 1950s and 1960s, when the lake's population of these fish was much bigger, commercial fishermen netted thousands of sharks and sawfish. Since the 1990s, however, the population of both sharks and sawfish have declined and catching one of them today is rare.

Timber is another natural resource. Valuable mahogany, ebony, and rosewood trees grow in the highlands, and the northern Atlantic area is rich in pines. The once-thriving timber industry is slowly recovering from the effects of Hurricane Mitch in 1998 and from changes in forestry management that come from shifting government policies.

About 16 percent, or 8,000 square miles (20,720 sq km), of the land is considered arable, or suitable for growing things. Of this land, roughly 1,000 square miles (about 2,590 sq km) are actively cultivated. Another large portion of the land is used for grazing cattle.

FLORA AND FAUNA

Many varieties of plants and animals are indigenous to Nicaragua and other Central American countries. Some of the plants and trees, such as cedar, oak, and pine, are just as easily found in Nicaragua as in countries in the north. However, because Nicaragua's climate varies from region to region, such tropical plants as tamarind and persimmon trees can also be found.

Many animal species found in North America also live in parts of Nicaragua. For example, deer, rattlesnakes, and coyotes are common in the highlands and in some sections of the western lowlands. As Nicaragua's climate is different than that in temperate countries, animals usually only seen in zoos inhabit areas of this tropical country, especially the jungles. These exotic animals include toucans, sloths, monkeys, jaguars, wild boars, and boa constrictors. Coral reefs are also found off the coasts.

INTERNET LINKS

www.history.com/this-day-in-history/earthquake-rocks-managua
"Earthquake Rocks Managua" revisits the 1972 disaster.

www.lonelyplanet.com/nicaragua/managua
Lonely Planet offers a lively overview of Managua.

vianica.com/attractions.php
This travel site has information on many of Nicaragua's natural features.

www.wired.com/2014/02/nicaragua-canal
Wired offers a report on the construction of the Nicaragua canal.

HISTORY

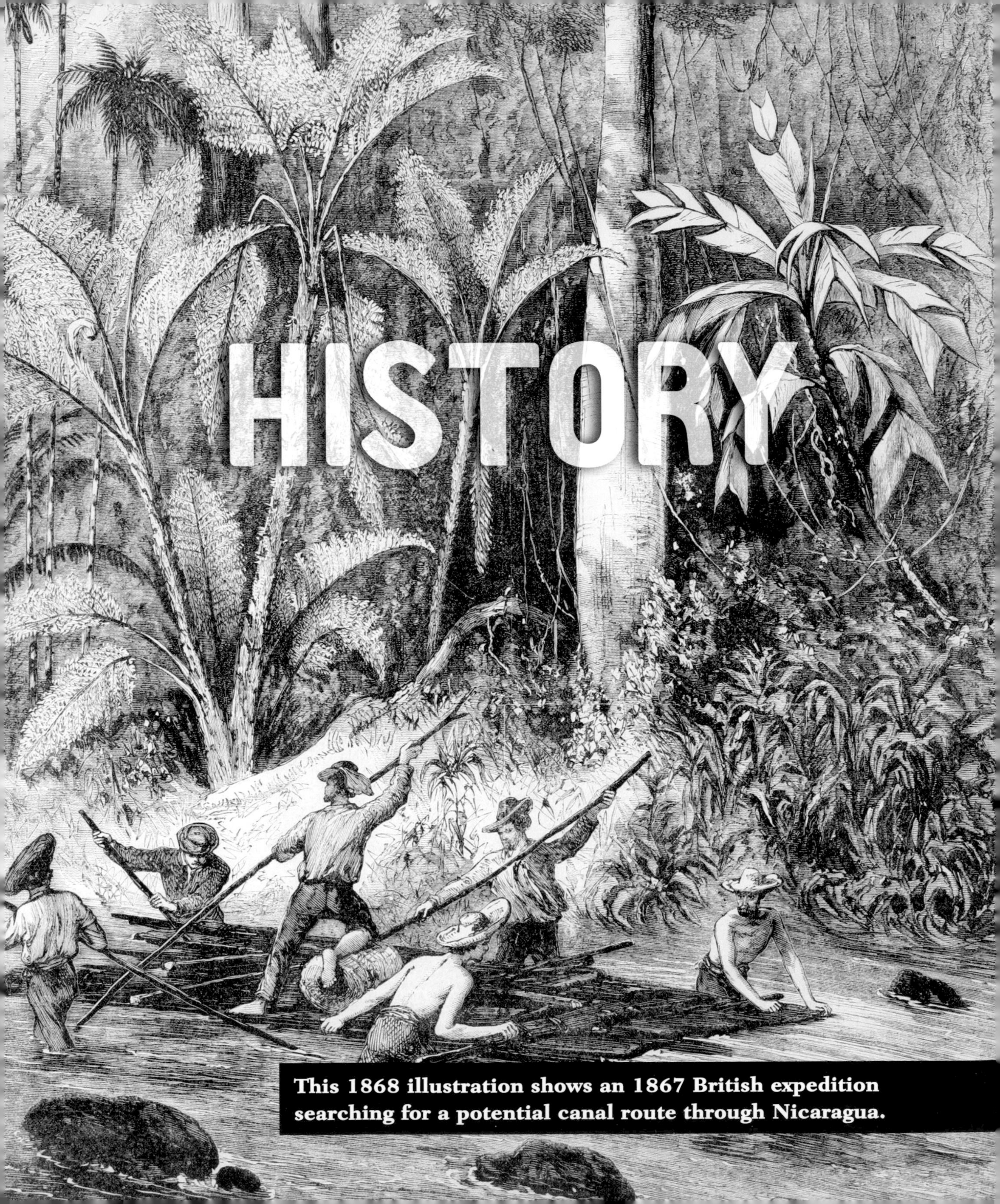

This 1868 illustration shows an 1867 British expedition searching for a potential canal route through Nicaragua.

2

THE COUNTRY OF NICARAGUA is relatively young. In 2021, it will observe the two hundredth anniversary of its independence from Spain. In 2038, Nicaragua will celebrate its bicentennial, or two hundredth birthday, as an independent republic.

Nicaraguans have been ruled by the Spanish, other Central American states, the US Marines, local dictators, a socialist regime, and most recently, a democratically elected president and National Assembly. As a republic, the nation survived almost thirty years of near anarchy, followed by several decades of dictatorship and two civil wars.

THE FIRST PEOPLE

The history of the land goes back much farther than two centuries, of course. Anthropologists and archaeologists have found evidence that people have lived in Nicaragua from about six thousand to ten thousand years ago.

The early people who settled in the west and center of the country were related to the Aztecs and Maya of Mexico. They probably found the fertile soils in the region suitable for growing food, and so settled in simple villages. Corn and beans were their main crops. One of the largest of these groups of people was the Nicarao, who inhabited much of the Pacific lowlands. Along the eastern coast, a group of ethnically different indigenous people hunted, fished, and practiced slash-and-burn agriculture. Their staple foods were root crops, such as cassava,

The name Nicaragua comes from Nicarao, the chief of the largest indigenous tribe in 1522. It means "here at the lake," referring to Lake Nicaragua.

In Granada, a statue honors the conquistador Francisco Hernández de Córdoba, the city's founder.

plantains, and pineapples. The indigenous people produced intricate works of art, especially pottery and gold jewelry. Religion and trading networks were important to their lives.

SPANISH RULE

After Christopher Columbus traveled to Central America and reported to the king of Spain that great wealth could be found there, many Spanish explorers set out for the New World in search of riches. One such explorer was the conquistador, or "conqueror," Gil González Dávila. In 1522, he became the first European to arrive in Nicaragua, but before he could form a settlement, the indigenous peoples chased him off the land.

One of Spain's earlier colonies was in Panama, where Pedro Arias de Ávila, or Pedrarias, became the ruler. He sent his lieutenant, Francisco Hernández de Córdoba, on a special mission to Nicaragua, and in 1523, Hernández landed in the country. He founded two cities, Granada and León, and went against Pedrarias' wishes by trying to make Nicaragua a separate Spanish province.

By Pedrarias' order, Hernández was beheaded, and Pedrarias became Nicaragua's governor from 1526 to 1531. He conquered the Nicaraguans just as he had conquered the indigenous people in Panama—by force. In fact, the Spaniards conquered large areas of Latin America, forcing its peoples to obey Spanish rules and customs, teaching them the Spanish version of world history, and replacing their religions with the Roman Catholic faith.

The leaders chosen to govern Nicaragua were often cruel to the indigenous groups. Natives had to work on the Spaniards' farms rather than farming their own land. Being forced to give up their traditions naturally made the Natives resentful of the government. A large number were sent to Peru and other Spanish colonies as slaves to work in mines. Mestizos, or people of mixed indigenous and Spanish descent, tried to avoid forced labor by adopting Spanish customs and denouncing their aboriginal heritage.

Between 1519 and 1650 about two-thirds of all indigenous people living in Central America lost their lives as a result of warfare, disease, and slavery. Those who survived were forced off their land because the *conquistadores* wanted to build cities there.

During the 1660s, the Spanish introduced a system of local government into Nicaragua. Property owners selected the members of a town council, and the position of council member was passed down from father to son. Usually these offices were held by residents of Spanish ancestry who were born in the colonies. People of Spanish ancestry were a privileged class in Nicaragua at the time. They controlled much of the trade and had the most political power. Spanish people lived pretty much as they pleased, while the indigenous people were treated harshly.

By the early nineteenth century, people across Central America had become unhappy with Spain's rule, which they saw as unjust. In 1821, Nicaragua and the rest of the Central American countries declared their independence.

INDEPENDENCE

After 1821, Nicaragua became part of the First Mexican Empire, but not for long. In 1823, Nicaragua left the empire to join the United Provinces of Central America, an organization of former Spanish colonies ruled by a central government in Guatemala City. Problems arose when Nicaraguan officials became unhappy with Guatemala's attempts at centralizing power. One major disagreement was over the building of a canal through Nicaragua. Nicaraguans saw the proposed canal as a way to increase the country's economic activity, but the central government decided it would take business away from ports in Guatemala. Eventually Nicaraguan officials decided the central government was too far away to understand their needs. In 1838, Nicaragua left the United Provinces and became an independent republic.

The United Provinces of Central America was soon renamed the Federal Republic of Central America. It was a sovereign state and a republican democracy that existed from 1823 to 1841. The nation was made up of the present-day countries of Guatemala, El Salvador, Honduras, Costa Rica, and Nicaragua. In the 1830s, an additional state was added, called Los Altos. It was made up of the western highlands of today's Guatemala and part of southern Mexico's state of Chiapas.

The founders of the new republic, led by Francisco Morazán of Honduras, believed Central America had a great future because it was an important trade route between the Atlantic and Pacific oceans. A federal president would govern from Guatemala City, and local governors would rule in each of the states.

The republic found it could not hold together politically, however, and civil war broke out from 1838 to 1840. Nicaragua separated from the union in 1838, and Honduras and Costa Rica quickly followed. These secessions prompted the disintegration of the union, which was made official in February 1841.

BRITISH INTEREST

In the late seventeenth century the Caribbean lowlands came under British influence. The British formed an alliance with one of the local aboriginal groups, the Miskito. The Miskito people later intermarried with slaves who had escaped from British plantations in the Caribbean. Between 1740 and 1786, the Mosquito Coast was a British dependency, and a struggle ensued between Spain and Britain for control of the region.

By the mid-1800s, Nicaragua had become a focal point for the United States and Britain, who were considering the creation of a passage across the isthmus to connect the Atlantic and Pacific oceans. Britain had consolidated its influence in the east with the departure of the Spanish and was eager to develop any possible riches inside Nicaragua. Fearing a British takeover, Nicaragua turned to the United States for protection. However, it was only during the presidency of José Santos Zelaya that the Mosquito Coast finally came under Nicaraguan jurisdiction.

THE TURNING POINT

In the eighteenth century two conflicting groups in Nicaragua had been formed. They differed on how the country should be run. In many ways, the two groups had similar goals, but they each had a different plan on how to achieve those goals. The group based in León became known as the Liberal Party; the other group, the Conservative Party, governed Granada. The Liberals favored political liberty, while the Conservatives favored political order and the ideas of the colonial past. This led to constant conflicts between the two groups that continues even today.

An American mercenary, William Walker, went to Nicaragua at the request of government officials in León. He was supposed to help them defeat Granada in a battle over which party would control the country, but after a bloody battle, Walker made himself president in 1856. For a year he ruled the country as an oppressive tyrant. Despite opposition from local leaders, he sold or gave land to US companies, declared English the official language, and legalized slavery. He also tried to make Nicaragua part of the United States.

Nicaragua's two warring parties joined forces and recruited many peasants to help fight Walker. The people of Nicaragua succeeded in overthrowing Walker and forced him to leave the country.

Once the two partisan groups had stopped fighting among themselves, they were able to form a centralized government. However, from 1857 to 1893, almost all the presidents were conservatives. They passed laws that made it harder for peasants to own land, essentially taking away the farmers' livelihood.

At the beginning of the nineteenth century, land was wealth, and most Nicaraguans owned at least some land. By 1900, however, distinct class boundaries had formed, dividing poor peasant farmers from the wealthy landowners for whom they worked.

US INVOLVEMENT

Around this time, the idea of building a canal to connect the two oceans reared its head once again. Zelaya, the liberal president who took office in

WALKER'S FILIBUSTER

William Walker (1824–1860) of Nashville, Tennessee, had a dream. He wanted to establish English-speaking colonies in Latin America, all of which would be under his direct control. Today that may sound like quite a radical—if not crazy—idea, but it wasn't unheard of at the time. During the nineteenth century, a number of Americans got involved in military schemes of their own making in Latin America. Such personal military meddling in other countries—a practice called filibustering—was, and is, illegal. But that didn't stop Walker.

He first tried to create a colony in the Baja California part of Mexico. In 1853, he and a group of mercenaries captured La Paz and declared it the Republic of Lower California, with himself as president. He then put the region under the laws of the US state of Louisiana, which made slavery legal. The expansion of slavery was one of Walker's goals, since he believed it was critical to a successful agrarian economy.

When Walker was overthrown and chased out of Mexico, he turned his attentions to Nicaragua. Taking advantage of the political strife in the region, Walker sailed to León in 1855 with about sixty like-minded Americans. With the consent of local Liberal Party officials, he and his troops set off to wipe out the party's Conservative political enemies in Granada. If the officials in León thought Walker would stop there, they were in for a surprise. Walker took over the entire country—again, with himself as president. He immediately launched an Americanization program, reinstated slavery, declared English an official language, and reorganized monetary policies to encourage immigration from the United States. Astonishingly, US President Franklin Pierce recognized Walker's regime as the legitimate government of Nicaragua. Walker actually had a great deal of US popular support, especially among Southerners.

Troops from neighboring Central American countries ousted Walker from Granada in 1856. As they fled, Walker's men burned the city to the ground. The following spring, Walker surrendered to the US Navy and returned to the United States. He couldn't leave Latin America alone, however, and returned there in 1860 with another scheme. This time, authorities in Honduras executed him by firing squad. William Walker was thirty-six years old.

1893, refused to grant the United States unrestricted rights to build the canal. Many Nicaraguans, especially conservatives, opposed Zelaya, a harsh dictator.

The United States encouraged the conservative opposition to revolt against Zelaya. When two US citizens who participated in the revolt were executed by Zelaya's officers, the United States decided it was time to take direct action. Four hundred US Marines were sent in to preserve order. Stationed in Bluefields on the Mosquito Coast, the Marines tried to block a liberal victory. When Zelaya resigned in 1909, another liberal, José Madriz, took his place. The United States also refused to recognize Madriz. The civil war in Nicaragua continued for several more months until conservative president Adolfo Díaz took office in 1911.

José Santos Zelaya

A brief period of relative calm followed. But then Díaz made an agreement that turned over control of the country's finances to the United States as a condition for a loan from US banks. The contract put the United States in charge of Nicaragua's finances until 1925, when the debt was paid off.

Soon the Marines were back, this time to deal with the forces that opposed US control. In 1916, a treaty was ratified to give the United States exclusive rights to build a canal and to establish naval bases. Although the United States later decided to build the canal in Panama, the naval bases were built in Nicaragua. The US Marines occupied Nicaragua almost continuously until 1933, protecting US interests and supervising elections.

THE FIRST SANDINISTAS EMERGE

Eventually, the opposition rallied together under General Augusto César Sandino, who led the rebels from 1927 to 1933. These rebels named themselves Sandinistas after their leader and adopted guerrilla tactics, with small groups hiding in the mountains and periodically ambushing to attack the US Marines.

The Sandinistas knew they were greatly outnumbered by the US Marines, but they fought anyway. General Sandino's motto was "Free homeland or

This portrait of General Anastasio Somoza ("Tacho") was taken in 1936, one year before he came to power.

death," and he often said, "It's better to die a rebel than to live as a slave."

Finally the United States decided to compromise. Instead of trying to impose democracy, it agreed to support any Nicaraguan leader who could promise peace in Nicaragua and friendship with the United States. In the 1932 election, the last supervised by the United States, a former rebel named Juan Bautista Sacasa became president.

The US Marines trained a new Nicaraguan army to help the president keep order. The handpicked head of this National Guard was a former used-car dealer and health inspector, Anastasio Somoza García.

In 1934, after the US Marines left Nicaragua, President Sacasa and General Sandino signed a peace treaty to end the fighting. However, Sandino also insisted the National Guard be dissolved. This led General Somoza to go behind the president's back and order the Guard to kill Sandino. The Guard also murdered more than three hundred of Sandino's supporters. When President Sacasa tried to take away General Somoza's control over the Guard, he discovered that General Somoza was much too powerful. In 1936, General Somoza forced President Sacasa (who was his uncle) to resign, and by the following year, the general was president of Nicaragua.

THE SOMOZA DYNASTY

For the next forty-two years (1937—1979), the Somoza family ruled the country. President Somoza, who was called "Tacho" by his friends and family, was eager to cooperate with the United States. He had its support because he was not a Communist and was powerful enough to prevent rebels from causing another war. Under his rule, the Nicaraguan government became stable enough for US corporations to start investing money in business prospects there. The economy expanded, but average Nicaraguans did not see the effects of this improvement.

Somoza had absolute power over the country's activities and used it to his personal advantage. When people tried to interfere with Somoza's authority, he had the National Guard threaten or kill them. He filled the Constituent Assembly with his supporters. The Assembly not only gave the president more powers, but in 1938, it also elected him for another eight-year term as president. In the 1940s, the United States persuaded Somoza not to run for another term. Somoza then appointed a family friend to the presidency. In 1950, Somoza again assumed the presidency. In 1956, at a ball in his honor, the poet Rigoberto López Pérez shot him dead in an attempt to end the dictatorship. It didn't work.

Somoza's eldest son Luis took over. During his five years in office, Luis tried to change the way the country was run, but in 1963, he was too ill to run for reelection. Instead, a close Somoza associate was elected president. In 1967 Luis died and his younger brother, Anastasio Somoza Debayle, won the elections that year. Somoza Debayle took over the country and ruled by his father's methods. Within a few years as president and head of the National Guard, he had increased his family's wealth to an estimated $900 million. The Somoza family owned one-fifth of the country's land, several sugar mills, factories, an airline, and several banks.

Somoza's two sons, photographed in 1937, are Anastasio Jr. (*left*), later called "Tachito," and Luis (*right*).

Anastasio Somoza Debayle, nicknamed Tachito, objected to being called a dictator. He argued that as he allowed the newspaper *La Prensa* to be published, he could not be a dictator. During the Somoza dynasty, however, less than half the population could read and a newspaper that criticized the government was not much of a threat as long as the majority of the governed could not read.

CIVIL WAR AND REVOLUTION

Reportedly, the blood plasma which arrived at the Managua airport to save the lives of earthquake victims in 1972 was promptly sold, for a profit, by a Somoza company to the United States.

By this time, a distinct upper class had developed. It included friends and supporters of the Somozas, corporate leaders who profited from Somoza Debayle's unethical economic regime, and a few successful independent business owners. The rest of the population was mostly poor, and they were becoming more aware of Somoza Debayle's corruption. Bands of guerrilla rebels began to form. In the early 1960s, the Sandinista National Liberation Front (FSLN) was founded, taking its name and some of its ideas from the rebels who fought under General Sandino in the 1920s. The FSLN members wanted Somoza Debayle out of office. They wanted to form a new government that would teach people to read and write, improve health care, provide food and housing, and give political power to workers and peasants. It was dangerous to be known as a Sandinista because the National Guard imprisoned or killed people whom they believed were associated with the FSLN.

Two events brought Somoza Debayle's abuse of power out into the open. First, in 1972, Somoza Debayle and his National Guard were accused of taking advantage of the terrible earthquake that destroyed Managua. Humanitarian aid poured in from all over the world, but very little of it actually made it into the hands of the people. Supplies, food, blankets, and medicines were allegedly confiscated by Somoza Debayle and his officers and resold for their own profit. (Somoza Debayle later wrote a book called *Nicaragua Betrayed*, in which he explained his side of the story. He denied all the accusations of corruption following the earthquake.)

As more people found out about Somoza Debayle's abuse of power, the FSLN gained popularity, even among the middle class and businesspeople. In 1974, after the FSLN kidnapped a few government officials, some of whom were Somoza Debayle's relatives, the National Guard launched a violent attack on the FSLN. Many FSLN members were killed, including one of its founders, José Carlos Fonseca Amador.

When the second event, the assassination of newspaper editor Pedro Joaquín Chamorro, occurred in January 1978, the public was outraged. Nicaraguans loved Chamorro because he stood up to Somoza Debayle and

In July 1979, Anastasio "Tachito" Somoza Debayle fled first to Miami but was denied entry to the United States by President Jimmy Carter. Somoza then went into exile in Paraguay, which was under the dictatorship of Alfredo Stroessner.

On September 17, 1980, Somoza was assassinated at age fifty-four near his home in Paraguay. He was ambushed in his car (shown here) by a seven-person Sandinista commando team (four men and three women). Later media reports stated that Somoza's body was so unrecognizable that forensics had to identify him through his feet.

Curiously, although he had been refused landing in Miami while he was alive, Somoza—what was left of him—ended up being buried there, care of some wealthy Nicaraguan exiles in South Florida.

printed articles in his newspaper, *La Prensa*, describing Somoza Debayle's corruption. Many people believed that the dictator had ordered Chamorro's murder. Thousands of demonstrators showed up at Chamorro's funeral.

In August 1978, the FSLN held the national palace hostage for two days. Although the crisis was eventually resolved, the National Guard responded by killing many civilians. The FSLN, in turn, captured many cities. Neighboring countries urged Somoza Debayle to resign. In July 1979, Somoza Debayle announced his resignation and fled the country. Up to fifty thousand Nicaraguans are believed to have died in the conflict to unseat him.

THE CONTRA WAR

The Sandinistas ruled Nicaragua from 1979 to 1990, with FSLN leader Daniel Ortega (b. 1945) serving as president from 1985 to 1990. They tried to help the poor and improve the economy, but after a brief period of improvement, a new civil war began to take its toll on the economy and hamper the Sandinistas' efforts at social reform.

By the early 1980s a new group of rebels had formed. They were called counter-revolutionaries (or Contras) because they had grown disillusioned with the revolution and opposed the changes the Sandinistas were trying to make. Some contras were former National Guard members who set up military bases in neighboring Costa Rica and Honduras, in order to conduct armed raids into Nicaraguan territory. The Contras were accused of committing atrocities, including widespread murder and torture, in an attempt to terrorize the population and destabilize the Sandinista government.

The US government supported the Contras. The US feared the Sandinistas were communists who would allow the Soviet Union to set up military bases in Nicaragua. The Sandinistas received money and military aid in the form of tanks, fighter aircraft, and helicopter gunships from the Soviet Union and Cuba, another communist country. Since US officials perceived this as a threat

Contra rebels dressed in camoflage uniforms

to US freedom and democracy, US president Ronald Reagan authorized military aid to the Contras, and in 1985 declared a trade embargo on Nicaragua. This took place despite 1982 Congressional legislation prohibiting the United States from supplying the Contras with arms to overthrow the Sandinista government.

During this time, the Sandinistas declared an official State of Emergency, which remained in place from 1982 to 1988. The government limited or eliminated many civil liberties and imposed strict control over the media. The Sandinistas also instituted a ruthless forced relocation of tens of thousands of Indians from their lands, committing a wide range of atrocities against the indigenous people. Some fifteen thousand innocent people were reportedly imprisoned or killed during this period.

Violetta de Barrios Chamorro takes office as the newly elected president in 1990.

AFTER THE WAR

The Contra War lasted until 1990, when a new president was elected. The winning campaign of Violeta de Barrios Chamorro, the first female president and widow of Pedro Chamorro, was endorsed by the United States because she planned to establish democracy in Nicaragua and introduce a free market economy. Although her years as president were marked by continued political struggles and economic problems, Chamorro initiated the creation of democratic institutions, worked toward national reconciliation, stabilized the economy, and reduced human rights violations. Doña Violeta, as Nicaraguans call her, became a beloved national figure.

In 1996, Nicaraguans elected a new president, former Managua mayor Arnoldo Alemán, and celebrated as power was peacefully transferred from one democratically elected president to another. Some important programs

President Daniel Ortega speaks at an International Workers Day ceremony at Revolution Square in Managua, in 2013.

were initiated during Alemán's years as president. However, the collapse of coffee prices and the devastation caused by Hurricane Mitch slowed the progress. In 2003, Alemán was convicted of embezzlement and sentenced to twenty years' imprisonment.

In 2001, Alemán's former vice-president, Enrique Bolaños, was elected president. Bolaños, the candidate for the ruling Liberal Constitutionalist Party (PLC), received 56 percent of the vote as compared to 42 percent for Daniel Ortega, leader of the FSLN. Bolaños promised to address poverty, unemployment, and corruption and also to seek relief from the country's burden of international debt. His goal of lowering the national debt was met in 2004 when the World Bank forgave 80 percent of the country's debt. Later that year Russia also agreed to forgive Nicaragua's debt, which dated back to the Soviet era.

ORTEGA RETURNS

In 2006, Daniel Ortega was once again elected president, with a mere 38 percent of the vote. In 2011, Ortega won yet another term, this time with 62.5 percent of the vote. During his terms, he has reached out to other socialist leaders in the Americas, such as Hugo Chavez of Venezuela and Luiz Inácio Lula da Silva of Brazil.

Ortega has instituted reforms to combat hunger and improve access to health care, education, credit, and social security. He is reportedly softening his former Marxist stance and leaning more toward social democracy. In recent years, Nicaragua has experienced economic growth and political stability.

However, Ortega's conservative Roman Catholicism has taken a stronger hold on his policies. In the 1980s, Ortega had been in favor of abortion rights, for example, but has since changed his mind. In Nicaragua, abortion is now completely illegal for any reason.

Though Ortega continues to criticize the United States, he supports and cooperates with US drug enforcement efforts in Central America. Under Ortega, drug-related activity and crime is lower in Nicaragua than in surrounding countries. In fact, Nicaragua has one of the lowest homicide rates in Central America.

Ortega's future in power will soon be put to the test. In 2014 the National Assembly approved changes to the constitution allowing Ortega to run for a third successive term.

INTERNET LINKS

america.aljazeera.com/opinions/2015/4/daniel-ortega-is-a-sandinista-in-name-only.html
An interesting article charges President Daniel Ortega with betraying his revolutionary roots.

news.bbc.co.uk/2/hi/americas/country_profiles/1225283.stm
BBC News offers a timeline of events in Nicaraguan history.

www.biography.com/people/daniel-ortega-40192
A quick overview of Daniel Ortega's life

vianica.com/go/specials/15-sandinista-revolution-in-nicaragua.html
This site offers an overview of the Sandinista Revolution

vianica.com/go/specials/16-augusto-sandino.html
This is a profile of Augusto Sandino.

GOVERNMENT

N ICARAGUA IS A PRESIDENTIAL representative democratic republic with multiple political parties. After surviving decades of armed conflict, US military intervention and occupation, rebellion, assassination, and dictatorships, the country seems to be settling into a calmer political climate. That said, Nicaragua remains a very poor country, which threatens political stability.

THE CONSTITUTION

Nicaragua's first constitution was written in 1838, when the country declared itself an independent nation. Since then, a number of other official constitutions have come and gone, reflecting the country's history and changing types of governments. In 1987, Nicaragua issued its ninth constitution, and that is the one in place today. However, since that time, there have been several amendments, or changes, added; the most recent one in 2014.

HUMAN RIGHTS The constitution guarantees civil liberties, including freedom of speech, the press, and religion; and guarantees the right to own land. The constitution prohibits discrimination based on birth, nationality, political belief, race, gender, language, religion, opinion, national origin, economic, or social condition.

3

The Nicaraguan flag has three horizontal bands behind the national coat of arms. The white band represents the land; the two blue bands signify the two oceans. In the coat of arms, the triangle stands for equality; the rainbow for peace; the red (Phrygian) cap for freedom; and the five volcanoes represent the five Central American countries.

minimum number of votes required to win an election. Previously, the winning candidate needed to receive at least 35 percent of the vote to be elected president. It also did away with a limit on how many consecutive terms a president could serve, effectively clearing the way for President Daniel Ortega to pursue a fourth overall and third consecutive term in 2016. The new constitution also allows the president to issue decrees with force of law and allows the appointment of active duty police and military officials to government offices which were previously set aside for civilians.

Ortega, who naturally supports the amendments, said the changes were needed for the stability of the nation. The opposition continues to argue that they are a threat to democracy.

THE BRANCHES OF GOVERNMENT

The government consists of three branches: the executive, the legislative, and the judicial.

THE PRESIDENT The position of president of Nicaragua was created in the Constitution of 1854. From 1825 until the Constitution of 1838 the title of the position was known as Head of State (*Jefe de Estado*) and from 1838 to 1854 as Supreme Director (*Director Supremo*).

In Nicaragua, the president is both chief of state and head of the government. Nicaraguans vote directly to elect the president for a five-year term, and anyone over sixteen can vote. The president appoints the Council of Ministers (the cabinet).

THE NATIONAL ASSEMBLY The National Assembly is the legislative, or law-making, branch of the government. It is a unicameral, or one-house, body, as it does not have two separate houses of representatives. It is made up of ninety elected representatives, the country's former president, and the runner-up in the presidential election, for a total of ninety-two representatives.

The country is divided into fifteen departments (much like provinces) and two autonomous regions. Based on their population, the departments and

regions get a certain number of representatives in the National Assembly. These representatives are elected by popular vote. Ministers of any church or religious organization are not allowed to serve in the Assembly.

THE JUDICIARY The judicial branch consists of several court districts spread out over the country, with each district representing several departments. The Supreme Court is in Managua, and the next highest courts are five Chambers of Second Instance, located in León, Granada, Masaya, Matagalpa, and Bluefields. The National Assembly elects the sixteen Supreme Court judges to five-year terms, based on a list of candidates submitted by the president. Judges of the lower courts are appointed by the Supreme Court.

POLITICAL PARTIES

The Sandinista National Liberation Front (Frente Sandinista de Liberación Nacional, FSLN) is a democratic socialist party. It is one of Nicaragua's tow

The Nicaraguan National Assembly meets in Managua on March 7, 2013, to honor the recently deceased president of Venezuela, Hugo Chavez.

Diplomatic relations between Nicaragua and the United States have been rocky. Nicaragua faults the United States for its aggressive intervention in the nineteenth and twentieth centuries, and for its support of the Somoza regimes. The United States, meanwhile, took a dim view of the Sandinista revolution, during which a great deal of private property was seized and redistributed by the revolutionary government. During the administration of President Ronald Reagan, US officials feared Nicaragua was becoming a communist country. The US support for the Contras in the 1980s marked a low point in the countries' bilateral relations.

Relations improved in 1990 with the introduction of democratic elections in Nicaragua. However, the United States charged that there were "significant irregularities" in the 2011 election that gave Daniel Ortega a second consecutive term. For his part, Ortega has been

A supporter of President Daniel Ortega holds a poster accusing the United States of imperialist aggression.

a vocal critic of the United States. If Ortega pursues and wins another presidential term in 2016, it may cause relations between the two countries to further disintegrate, but that also depends on what direction US politics take as well. Despite political divisiveness, both countries are active trade partners and maintain diplomatic embassies.

leading parties. This party grew out of the Sandinista movement that overthrew Anastasio Somoza Debayle in 1979. The FSLN then established a revolutionary government which ruled from 1979 to 1990. This is the party of Daniel Ortega.

The Constitutionalist Liberal Party (Partido Liberal Constitucionalista, PLC) is the main opposition party to the FSLN. This is the party of both former presidents Arnoldo Alemán and Enrique Bolaños, though Bolaños went on to form a new party, the Alliance for the Republic. This party is a right-wing liberal-conservative party backed by some of the country's most affluent capitalists.

Supporters of the Sandinista National Liberation Front (FSLN) wave party flags during the celebration of the anniversary of the Sandinista Revolution, at La Fe square in Managua on July 19, 2012.

INTERNET LINKS

www.bbc.com/news/world-latin-america-15544315
BBC News offers this "Profile: Nicaraguan President Daniel Ortega."

www.cia.gov/library/publications/the-world-factbook/geos/nu.html
The CIA World Factbook lists up-to-date facts relating to Nicaragua's government.

www.constituteproject.org/constitution/Nicaragua_2005.pdf
A full English-language version of Nicaragua's 1987 Constitution is available here, but it includes amendments only through 2005.

nicaragua.usembassy.gov/econ_links.html
The US Embassy in Managua lists the official websites of the Nicaraguan government here, but note that all are available in Spanish only.

ECONOMY

Coffee beans, such as these at a farm in Diriamba, are an important Nicaraguan export.

4

I N RECENT YEARS, THE ECONOMIC news out of Nicaragua has been good. This is in contrast to the very bad economic times the country suffered through the last half-century. The long Somoza dictatorship weakened the economy, as did several natural disasters. Then, the Sandinista Revolution, coupled with the Contra War and a subsequent economic blockade by the United States in 1985, made for very hard times indeed.

Still reeling from those years, Nicaragua remains the second poorest nation in the Americas, after Haiti. Poverty and unemployment are widespread. About 40.5 percent of Nicaraguans live beneath the poverty level, and nearly 10 percent live in extreme poverty on less than $1 a day. In addition, more than 80 percent of Nicaragua's poor live in rural areas—many in remote communities where access to basic services is a daily challenge. In 2014, unemployment stood at 7.4 percent, but underemployment—which economists say is a much more revealing figure—was a troubling 46.5 percent as recently as 2008.

Nevertheless, Nicaraguans have reason for optimism.

About one million Nicaraguans work abroad and send a good portion of their wages home to their families. These monies are called remittances. They are a major source of Nicaragua's income, contributing to about 15 percent of the country's GDP.

A man collects
coffee beans at
El Puma Farm
outside Jinotega,

AGRICULTURE AND FISHERIES

Nicaragua is primarily an agricultural country. Revenue from agriculture makes up nearly 15 percent of the country's GDP and about 31 percent of the country's workforce does some type of agricultural work. Nicaragua grows the majority of its own food, and most of the farming is subsistence farming. That is, the farmer produces just enough food to feed the family. There is seldom a surplus to sell, so the family is stuck in poverty. Bad weather or bad luck can quickly lead to hunger.

One problem with agriculture has been the issue of land ownership. After taking office in 1990, the Chamorro administration reversed the Sandinistas' policy of nationalizing land by returning it to its original owners. However, the process of returning land to previous owners is a complicated issue, as it deprives the poor of essential farmland, while previous owners may have received their land through connections with powerful dictators. Achieving the right balance between private land ownership and popular demands for a right to land based on need is one of the nation's most pressing challenges.

Some of Nicaragua's most important fruits are bananas, pineapples, plantains, and oranges. Other important crops include sugarcane, rice, corn, sesame, dry beans, cotton, cocoa beans, and coffee.

COFFEE Nicaragua's largest agricultural export item is coffee. Billions of pounds of coffee are sold to the United States, Europe, and Japan. In 2014, Nicaragua was the fifteenth largest coffee producer in the world, growing 86,000 tons (78,000 metric tons) of beans. Ninety-five percent of Nicaragua's coffee is considered "shade grown." The Matagalpa region is said to produce the country's top quality coffee, while the neighboring Jinotega region produces 80 percent of its total crop.

More than 45,000 families own and operate small coffee plantations. Some have formed "fair trade" cooperatives, such as the Central de Cooperativas de Servicios Múltiples (PRODECOOP) in Estelí and Palacagüina, Nicaragua, which sell their beans to specialty roasters in the United States and Europe.

MEAT AND FISH In other agricultural sectors, beef cattle production has grown steadily since 1998 and is now almost as important as coffee as an export item. Veal, pork, and poultry are also exported.

Fisheries are also a growing sector of the economy. Nicaragua is the largest producer of seafood in Central America, with aquaculture shrimp being its leading product for export. Shrimp is farmed in the estuaries of Nicaragua's Pacific Coast. Lobsters and fish are also important exports. Some 94 percent of Nicaragua's seafood catch is exported.

INDUSTRY

Although Nicaragua remains heavily dependent on agriculture, agriculture's share of GDP has been decreasing steadily in recent years, while industry and services have been increasing. Industry now contributes 28.8 percent and

FREE TRADE VERSUS FAIR TRADE

The Dominican Republic–Central American Free Trade Agreement (CAFTA-DR) is a trade arrangement between the United States and the Central American countries of Costa Rica, El Salvador, Guatemala, Honduras, and Nicaragua, as well as the Dominican Republic. The agreement, approved in the United States in 2005 under the administration of President George W. Bush, is similar to the North American Free Trade Agreement (NAFTA), which exists between the United States, Canada, and Mexico.

These trade agreements reduce tariffs and trade restrictions between member countries. Free trade is meant to make exporting and importing more profitable for the nations involved. The United States also sees it as a way to create economic opportunity and help promote democracy in these countries. Some supporters see CAFTA-DR as a stepping stone toward an eventual Free Trade Area of the Americas (FTAA), which would also encompass South American and Caribbean nations.

Protestors in Managua wave anti-American signs during an anti-CAFTA rally in 2005.

Critics charge that the pact opens a country's economy to global competition, which can put its own industries at a disadvantage. They worry, therefore, that factory workers might see their wages lowered, for example, and that small farmers could be pushed aside to make way for more industrial-style farming. Opponents also say that free trade encourages companies to relocate to countries where environmental standards are not enforced. Opponents in Central America warned of a long list of negative outcomes when CAFTA-DR was being negotiated, and said the agreement skews heavily in favor of the United States.

Nevertheless, since CAFTA-DR, Nicaragua has seen record levels of growth in trade and investment. Nicaragua's exports to the United States grew 75 percent in the six years after its passage. Nicaragua now boasts more than $1 billion in trade surplus with the United States, thanks in large part to the trade agreement.

Though Sandinista Front initially attempted to block the trade agreement, saying it would be a "death certificate" for farmers and small producers, the ruling party has since reconsidered. Daniel Ortega's government recognizes CAFTA's role in attracting foreign investment, boosting exports, and generating employment.

Those who feel free trade is unfair to Nicaraguan workers and bad for the environment have proposed an alternative called fair trade. Fair trade is built on the premise that some customers are willing to pay a higher price for products that are manufactured using methods that do not degrade the environment and that give the workers a good wage and good working conditions. Many specialty coffee products from Nicaragua are sold with a fair trade label.

the service sector nearly 56.4 percent to Nicaragua's GDP. In 2014, Nicaragua saw its industrial production grow by 9 percent.

Food processing is one of the country's major industries. Export commodities also include textiles, clothing, cigars, and automobile parts. Leather, wood products, and cardboard cartons are other export items. Petroleum refining and distribution is also a major industry.

MINING In 2013, gold became Nicaragua's number one export, replacing coffee which has traditionally held that position. That year, Nicaragua's gold production showed an increase of 16.5 percent over the previous year, and generated $430 million in revenues. Gold is extracted from mines in the Northern Atlantic Autonomous Region and in the central highlands. Nicaragua's largest gold mine is in La Libertad and is owned by a Canadian company. When the price of gold is high internationally, gold mining means jobs for local men. However, the price of this metal fluctuates and in times of lower prices, miners find themselves without work.

Chinese businessman Wang Jing (*center*), representatives of the Nicaraguan government, and members of the Commission of the Grand Inter-Oceanic Canal attend the inauguration of the project in Tola, Nicaragua, in December 2014.

BETTING ON THE CANAL

Long-term success for Nicaragua requires attracting new businesses, creating jobs, and reducing poverty. Nicaragua must improve the country's infrastructure, such as roads, overcome corruption, resolve property rights issues, and continue to increase its foreign trade.

To this end, the government is betting the country's future on a project of grand proportion—the Nicaragua Interoceanic Grand Canal. Work on the proposed canal, described on page 15, broke ground in 2015. The administration of President Daniel Ortega originally claimed the huge project would bring up to a million jobs to Nicaragua. It is being called the largest engineering venture in history. The government sees this monumental endeavor as the "golden egg" that will change substantially and permanently improve the economy.

The future job prospects have since been estimated at fifty thousand per year for five years. Up to half of those employed would be Nicaraguan, according to the Chinese billionaire who is behind the project. The remaining workers would be 25 percent Chinese and 25 percent from other countries, because Nicaragua lacks enough skilled workers to fill management, training, and equipment operation spots.

There is tremendous controversy surrounding the canal, based on substantial environmental concerns. Whether these and other complicating issues will interrupt the project remains to be seen. While the Ortega government is betting on the canal, it's telling that only the Nicaragua Grand Canal Commission is projecting Nicaragua's economic growth related to the canal project. The International Monetary Fund and other global economic groups do not include the canal in their estimates for the country's future.

Nicaraguan demonstrators march against the canal, claiming it will hurt the environment.

INTERNET LINKS

projects.aljazeera.com/2015/04/nicaragua-canal
Al Jazeera America presents a five-part series on Nicaragua's canal project, with excellent photographs.

www.cia.gov/library/publications/the-world-factbook/geos/nu.html
The CIA World Factbook section on Nicaragua's economy has up-to-date facts and statistics.

nicaragua.usembassy.gov/econ_cafta.html
The US Embassy in Managua offers the US perspective of CAFTA-DR's benefits to Nicaragua.

ENVIRONMENT

A black-handed spider monkey, an endangered animal, appears to pose for a picture.

5

NICARAGUA IS CENTRAL AMERICA'S largest nation. It's also the region's least populated country and the one with the greatest amount of fresh water. Vast areas are covered in rain forest containing a rich diversity of plant and animal life. Given these facts, Nicaragua should be in an advantaged position in terms of environmental health.

Lake Laguna de Apoyo is a volcanic crater lagoon on Nicaragua's Pacific Coast.

Nicaragua has made great progress in access to drinking water, but there are still disparities between urban and rural areas. Only about 37 percent of the rural population has sanitation services, compared to 63 percent in the cities. A lack of water and sanitation affects a community's health, education, and productivity.

Cows graze in a pasture cleared from forest.

However, powerful forces have converged in a way that has damaged the land, water, and air. The country's political and economic problems, combined with frequent natural disasters, have made it difficult for the country to effectively protect the environment. Deforestation and water concerns are the most urgent problems.

The conversion of forests to agricultural land (for commercial agriculture and cattle pastures) and substantial logging with little or no government regulation are having a severe environmental impact. The country's Atlantic region has an area the size of El Salvador that is largely untouched and preserved. This is due more to the land's remoteness, with poor access and infrastructure, than to vigilant oversight. Even in many of the protected nature areas, illegal logging, poaching, and squatting are growing problems.

The western lowlands, meanwhile, on the Pacific side, have a poor record environmentally. In fact, the tiny crater Lake Tiscapa in the center of Managua is known locally as "the toilet." Lake Managua is heavily polluted, and Lake Nicaragua, the country's jewel, has lost almost all of its famous freshwater bull sharks.

CONSERVATION

During the Somoza years, little thought was given to protecting the environment. Instead, the dictatorship wanted to take advantage of the country's resources to gain wealth. As a result, some of Nicaragua's lakes and rivers were polluted with pesticides, raw sewage, and industrial waste, and many of the forests were cut down.

Under the Sandinistas, the government started extensive programs to restore and protect the environment. Many of these programs, while they sounded good, turned out to be inefficient and not very well thought out. Governments since then have tried to find the right balance, but progress is slow. Fortunately, many nongovernmental organizations (NGOs) have stepped in to support Nicaragua's efforts to conserve its natural resources. NGOs such as the World Wildlife Fund and the Nature Conservancy provide experts to work on scientific studies and money to pay for park rangers and equipment. NGOs also help fund educational projects that teach Nicaraguans the importance of protecting the environment.

Tourists visit the Masaya Volcano at Nicaragua's first and largest national park,

In recent years, six natural reserves—two in the mountains and four in the Pacific region—received special funding from the international community to improve their management. The goal was to find a way to start managing these reserves cooperatively because Nicaragua's government does not have the funds or expertise to manage them on its own.

Although money and technology may be lacking, the Nicaraguan government is aware of the issues it faces. The Ministry of Environment and Natural Resources is in charge of regulating and protecting the country's environment. Nicaragua has joined other countries in addressing the global challenge of environmental protection. Local and national governments and international groups, such as the United Nations and the World Bank, are working to help conserve Nicaragua's habitat, marine resources, and aquatic life.

ECOTOURISM

Around fifty years ago, Nicaragua's neighbor, Costa Rica, devoted much time and effort to protect its mountains and cloud forest habitats. Now it is considered one of the world's top nature destinations. Nicaragua, on the other hand, fought civil wars and suffered poverty during the same period. As a result, it has not enjoyed much tourism, and the government now wants to change that. It sees tourism as a path out of poverty and is encouraging the growth of eco-friendly tourism. Ecotourism brings in jobs and money, and it serves to protect wildlife habitats. Visitors can hike through wildlife-filled rain forests, climb sulfur-spitting volcanoes, spend a few nights at a lodge located in the forest, and roam miles of undeveloped shoreline knowing that

LAKE NICARAGUA–RÍO SAN JUAN WATERSHED

The lands of the Lake Nicaragua–Río San Juan watershed include numerous types of ecosystems (a watershed is the region of land where the water drains into a specified body of water). The areas to the east, north, and west of Lake Nicaragua are covered with dry tropical forest. This important lower-elevation habitat has a large variety of trees, and many of them shed their leaves during the dry season. At one time, dry tropical forest covered much of Central America's Pacific coast from Mexico to Panama, but most of it has been cut down for agricultural use.

South and southwest of Lake Nicaragua, the land receives more rain. Here, in the tropical rain forest, palms and ferns grow alongside an amazing variety of tree species, some growing to great heights. Other species grow below the tallest trees in a series of green layers. Mahogany and cedar are common, but dozens of other lesser-known species also occur here.

A part of the San Juan watershed extends across the border into Costa Rica. Here the watershed includes the upper elevations of a volcanic mountain range, and at the top of these mountains is a cloud forest. Cloud forests are wet and are covered in fog and clouds most of the time. These highlands have an abundance of moss, ferns, and plants called epiphytes that grow on trees. Orchids are the most well-known type of epiphytes.

Along the banks of the Río San Juan grows a special type of forest called gallery forest. Here ficus, balsa wood, and other species of trees thrive in the humid conditions, and they can withstand periodic flooding. In the shallow, fresh water along the lakes, rivers, and estuaries of the watershed, fragile wetlands harbor many species of aquatic birds and provide nesting places for fish, reptiles,

Ridley sea turtle hatchlings scurry to the ocean.

and amphibians. Finally, where the watershed meets the sea, mangrove swamps flourish in flooded coastal areas; these highly specialized ecosystems are home to a high number of saltwater-loving animal species, such as the mangrove crab. Usually the only trees in these swamps are the low-growing, evergreen mangroves, which are well adapted to their salty and swampy habitat.

the money they spend on their visit is helping to preserve what they are enjoying.

A number of new tourism projects are designed to help local people directly. Not only do tourists get to enjoy the pristine environment and beauty of Nicaragua's natural areas, but their money provides work and a stable income for local residents, as well as enabling local children to attend school.

Tourism also has its disadvantages—mainly crowds and high prices. Relatively untouched by tourism and development, the current condition of Nicaragua's Miraflor Nature Reserve is said to be just like Costa Rica's cloud forests fifty years ago.

A male resplendent quetzal displays its exotic coloring in flight.

NATURE RESERVES

Nicaragua holds a vital place in what biologists call the Mesoamerican Biological Corridor. A biological corridor is an area of land that connects habitats over a long distance. Mesoamerica is an area of land that stretches from southern Mexico to Panama. It covers just 0.5 percent of Earth's land area, but is home to nearly 10 percent of the world's known species. Monkeys, harpy eagles, and several species of sea turtles still live here. American manatees, Central American tapirs, Central American woolly opossums, giant anteaters, and Honduran fruit-eating bats are some of the other endangered animals living in this area.

Nicaragua is striving to protect as much of its natural heritage as it can. Nicaragua currently has more than seventy protected areas; the most important either protect remaining large areas of undeveloped land or target specific endangered species or habitats. For example, the 128-square-mile (150 sq km) Miraflor Nature Reserve harbors the legendary bird of Central America, the quetzal, plus three hundred species of orchids, beautiful waterfalls, and monkeys.

In Rivas, people enjoy a dip in Lake Nicaragua. The inhabitants of the area are mostly opposed to the construction of the canal.

AN ENVIRONMENTAL CATASTROPHE?

In recent years, a new environmental threat has arisen. The government's 2014 commitment to the building of a trans-oceanic canal has raised many issues of concern. Among the most pressing questions are those relating to the impact such a gargantuan project will have on Nicaragua's already stressed environment.

In particular, many scientists say the canal could have a catastrophic effect on Lake Nicaragua. Also called Lake Cocibolca, it's the second largest lake in Latin America, with an area of 3,149 square miles (8,156 sq km), and it's the principal water reservoir for Nicaragua and Central America.

The canal will cross through the lake, which will greatly increase traffic. Massive ships capable of carrying 12,500 containers and measuring a quarter of a mile long will traverse the lake every day. To be able to accommodate such ships, the lake will need to have an enormous amount of soil dredged from its bottom. Scientists worry that pollution and sedimentation will destroy the lake's life forms. Sedimentation is the stirring up and resettling of the lakebed materials. The process damages water quality by decreasing oxygen levels and light penetration. Lake Nicaragua is naturally vulnerable to sedimentation because it is both shallow and windy, making sediments that settle on the lake floor easy to stir up.

The lake's health is just one of many environmental fears the canal project raises. The proposed route crosses protected areas of rain forests, wetlands, and nature reserves. It will require the clearing of hundreds of thousands of acres of forests and wetlands, which will disrupt the migration patterns of animals. Several endangered species live in these regions, including tapirs, spider monkeys, harpy eagles, and jaguars.

Critics say the country's laws are inadequate to ensure that the construction will not harm the land, and furthermore, they say, the laws don't hold the Chinese company building the canal accountable for ecological damage. The company, for its part, insists the canal will be built to international safety standards.

A crowded passenger ferry on Lake Nicaragua approaches the dock on Ometepe Island.

INTERNET LINKS

projects.aljazeera.com/2015/04/nicaragua-canal/environment.html
This is an excellent article on the ecosystem of Lake Nicaragua, the fishing community that depends on it, and the potential environmental damage that the new canal could cause.

www.nicaragua.com/national-parks
This is a quick listing of the national parks in Nicaragua, with short descriptions.

toursnicaragua.com
ToursNicaragua is one of several sites that offer ecotours, with photos and descriptions.

www.worldbank.org/en/news/feature/2013/01/22/agua-saneamiento-comunidades-rurales
The World Bank has a short report on the state of Nicaragua's water and sanitation.

NICARAGUANS

A Nicaraguan girl smiles for the camera.

NICARAGUANS, OR NICAS, AS THEY are called, are a people of different ethnicities and races. In fact, they are mostly a mixed-race people, the result of five hundred years of cultural interaction. They are typically friendly and generous people who keep their spirits up despite their nation's many economic and political problems.

Even in the worst situations, someone who has food will usually share with someone who is hungry, and Nicaraguans never hesitate to open their homes to visitors. They generally display a strong pride in their homeland, and their nationality is very important to them.

Nicaraguans have different ethnic origins. Most are *mestizos*, people of mixed Spanish and indigenous ancestry, but several other ethnic groups make up the rest of the population: indigenous peoples, Creoles, black Caribs, and Spaniards. Most of the indigenous groups, Creoles, and blacks live in the eastern part of Nicaragua, while the western part is inhabited mainly by mestizos. Nicaragua's geography makes it hard to get from one coast to the other, so people identify more with the region they live in than with the nation as a whole. The distance between the two coasts has resulted in regional loyalties and characteristics.

There is a small Middle Eastern-Nicaraguan community living in Nicaragua. The people are of Syrian, Armenian, Palestinian, Jewish, and Lebanese descent and number about thirty thousand.

6

ETHNIC GROUPS

Six minority groups live mainly along the Atlantic Coast: Miskitos, Ramas, and Sumos (also known as Sumus) are aboriginal people whose ancestors were natives of the land before Spanish colonization; Creoles are of mixed European and African descent; and Garífunas and black Caribs have a mix of indigenous and African ancestry. Although the remote nature of the Atlantic Coast makes it hard to conduct an accurate census of the area, estimates from 2003 place Nicaragua's minority, or non-mestizo, population at about 14 percent, and most of these minorities live on the Atlantic Coast.

Nearly 70 percent of the indigenous people are Miskitos (the name is not related to the insect with a similar name, mosquito). In the seventeenth and eighteenth centuries, the Miskito nation expanded by conquering other aboriginal people. By 1850 they occupied the entire Mosquito Coast, which extends from Panama in the south to Honduras in the north. In the past, Miskitos practiced small-scale farming and fishing, as well as performing some seasonal salaried labor for foreign-owned companies. Today Miskitos are involved in local government and work in most sectors of the economy.

Around ten thousand Sumos live in small isolated communities along the coast and in a few larger villages in the Bambana River basin. Many Sumo communities were taken over by the Miskitos in the seventeenth and eighteenth centuries. An even smaller group is the Rama, only about four thousand of whom still live in Nicaragua. They live on Rama Cay, a small island in the Bay of Bluefields, and in Monkey Point, a village south of Bluefields. In the eighteenth century, they moved frequently to avoid being captured by Miskitos and sold to the British as slaves.

Around 25 percent of the non-mestizo population in Nicaragua have some African ancestry, and most of them live on the Atlantic Coast. Black Caribs first came to the area as slaves from British colonies in the West Indies. They

Like this boy, most Nicaranguan people are ethnically mestizo.

remained there after slavery was abolished in 1824 and today live mainly in the Laguna de Perlas area.

Creoles are people of African and Spanish, or other European, descent whose ancestors came from the West Indies to Nicaraguagua to work as indentured laborers on British plantations. When the British lost control of the region, many Creoles stayed. Around the same time, Jamaican merchants began arriving on the coast. In the nineteenth century, US lumber and banana companies attracted black workers from the southern United States and the Caribbean. Today most Creoles live in Bluefields and the surrounding area. Many are skilled or semiskilled workers, and some are office employees, technicians, or professionals.

Garífunas are a people of mixed Carib, Angolan, Congolese, and Arawak descent. They are black in physical appearance, but their culture derives from several Latin American indigenous groups. Their ancestors lived on the islands of St. Vincent and Dominica until the second Carib War (1795—1797). After the war, the British sent the survivors to an island in the Bay of Honduras. Over half the people died during the trip; only about two thousand arrived safely. Later, the Garífunas migrated to Nicaragua for better jobs in the mahogany industry and on banana plantations. Most of the three thousand Garífunas in Nicaragua today live at Laguna de Perlas and Bluefields.

A young man plays basketball in Bluefields.

CULTURAL DIFFERENCES

Nicaragua's two coasts are like two separate countries. People on one side know little about life on the other. The natural resources of the two areas are quite different, resulting in dissimilar lifestyles. Farmers on the Pacific side of the country know a lot about growing coffee and corn, while those in the east grow mainly coconuts and bananas. The main industries along the Caribbean coast are fishing and catching lobsters. On the Pacific Coast there are many more schools, colleges, and businesses. In the east, many indigenous people still follow the traditions and customs of their ancestors.

The people who live on the Caribbean are called *costeños* (koh-STEN-nohs; which means coastal people) by the residents of the Pacific side of Nicaragua, but sharing a name does not mean these diverse groups of people share a culture. Each group has its own language, culture, and traditions, all of which are a mystery to most of the residents of western Nicaragua. The *costeños* do not know much about the people from the Pacific side of the country either. They call them Spaniards, and worry that more and more will move to the east and bring with them their language, music, and food, diluting the *costeños*' cultural traditions.

Ethnic identity became an important issue only recently. Past governments mostly ignored the Caribbean coast, but when the Sandinistas came to power, they guaranteed civil rights for the non-mestizos and made ethnic identity a political issue. They promoted respect for traditional indigenous religions, languages, and celebrations but sometimes offended the indigenous people by trying to integrate them with the rest of Nicaragua. What the indigenous people really wanted was independence and control of the abundant natural resources in the region. Peace between the government and the indigenous people came when the Sandinistas helped organize an autonomous local government to regulate life on the Caribbean coast.

SOCIAL STRUCTURE

Throughout the twentieth century, distinct social classes existed in Nicaraguan culture. During the Somoza dictatorship, a very small upper class owned almost 80 percent of the land, while the rest of the people were poor, landless, and struggling to feed their families. In the 1970s over half the people earned only $250 each year. People were very rich or very poor; there was virtually no middle class.

After the revolution, the Sandinistas tried to shrink the gap between the rich and the poor by redistributing land confiscated from large landowners to peasants. However, the Contras specifically targeted and attacked farms and other food production facilities, destroying the Sandinistas' efforts. In the last twenty-five years, the country has tried to make capitalism work, and many wealthy upper-class people have gotten their land back.

Over the last decade or so, a fairly large middle class has emerged, consisting of families who have the basic necessities and maybe a few luxuries, such as a refrigerator or relatively new clothes. Usually, these families need two incomes to maintain their lifestyle. Most Nicaraguans would probably be considered working class, which means they have to work hard just to make ends meet. They are not poor, but they earn only enough money to buy food and other essentials. Many other people in the country still live in poverty.

How much power and opportunity people have usually depends on their job. Farmers usually do not have much political power, and they do not have many opportunities to advance to a higher social standing. The Sandinistas tried unsuccessfully to change this fact of Nicaraguan life, but the main factor that determines what kind of jobs people will have is the family they are born into. Many families have been poor for generations, and they often feel that there is no way to change their lives.

Unfortunately, this is usually true. It is hard for children of poor farmers to grow up to be wealthy business owners, for example. Often they do not finish school in order to help with the farm work. Children born to wealthy parents, on the other hand, have a much better chance of attending private schools or finishing their education in foreign countries. In Nicaragua, wealth equals power, and power brings opportunity, just as it does everywhere.

The people of the Corn Islands, off the Mosquito Coast, are predominantly an African-descended, English-speaking Creole people mixed with indigenous, European, Asian, and Arab heritage.

LEAVING THEIR HOMELAND

Although Nicaraguans possess a strong love of their homeland, economic problems and natural calamities have induced many to seek refuge in other countries. The effects of Hurricane Mitch and the fall of coffee prices in the late 1990s sent a large influx of Nicaraguans across the border into Costa Rica in search of work. By 2005, perhaps as many as 1,500,000 Nicas were living outside of their country, both legally and illegally.

Earlier, between 1979 and 1990, some 5 to 15 percent of the population left Nicaragua because of conflicts between the government and opposition forces. (Estimates vary greatly because some include only refugees and exiles, while others also count the Contras and their families who left when the Sandinistas took over.) Contra attacks along the Caribbean coast caused about forty thousand Miskitos and Sumos to flee to Costa Rica and Honduras.

Some Nicaraguans went to other Central American countries and some to Europe. Some moved to various parts of the United States, where by far the largest concentration of Nicaraguan ex-pats is in Miami.

A Nicaraguan man (left) applies for US citizenship in Miami.

LIFE IN MIAMI Nearly eighty thousand Nicaraguan Americans live in the Miami area. The Nicaraguan communities are made up of different cultures, just like in Nicaragua. There are mestizos, Creoles, and Miskitos, each with their own communities and organizations. Echoing the situation in Nicaragua, these communities do not have much contact with each other. The timing and reasons behind their arrival in Miami are different, too. Many of the Creole population came to study in the United States as early as the 1950s. The Miskitos, on the other hand, fled Nicaragua during the Contra War, when they were mistreated by both sides. Large numbers of mestizos lived in Miami even before the revolution of 1979.

José Martin, orginally from Nicaragua, drinks a soda in the Little Havana neighborhood of Miami.

INTERNET LINKS

www.famousbirthdays.com/birthplace/nicaragua.html
Some of Nicaragua's famous people are listed here.

www.ticotimes.net/2014/08/27/nicaraguan-migrants-dont-follow-other-central-americans-to-us-choosing-costa-rica-instead
This very interesting article explores the motivations and experiences of Nicaraguan migrants.

vianica.com/go/specials/6-racial_groups_Nicaragua.html
This article explores the racial makeup of the Nicaraguan people.

vianica.com/go/specials/32-current-indigenous-communities-of-nicaragua.html
The same website offers an in-depth look at the country's indigenous communities.

LIFESTYLE

Two brothers goof around in their living room.

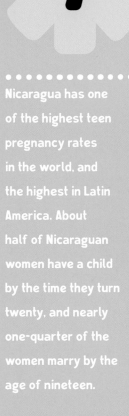

7

NICARAGUA IS A DEVELOPING country. As a whole, the nation's lifestyle levels lag behind those of industrialized nations. The country's history of tyranny and war prevented progress in many ways for decades. Recently, however, peace and government stability have improved the lives of many citizens.

LIVING CONDITIONS

About three-quarters of Nicaraguans live in cities, and every day many more are exchanging rural living for the urban life. Many people move to the cities, especially Managua, hoping to find better jobs. There are eight large cities. The three largest are Managua (population 2,223,000), León (population 201,000), and Chinandega (population 126,400). Other cities include Granada, Masaya, Matagalpa, Estelí, and Jinotepe.

Most cities have well-planned residential areas with gardens, parks, a market, and shopping centers, but nearly all of them also have barrios, or poorer neighborhoods where houses are crowded with people, small, and close together. One can usually tell how much money a family has by looking at the floor of their home. Poor people have dirt floors, while working- and middle-class people have cemented or tiled ones. Nearly half the people who are capable of working cannot find jobs or are underemployed; that is, they work at jobs that do not completely utilize their skills.

Nicaragua has one of the highest teen pregnancy rates in the world, and the highest in Latin America. About half of Nicaraguan women have a child by the time they turn twenty, and nearly one-quarter of the women marry by the age of nineteen.

GETTING AROUND AND STAYING IN TOUCH

Until recently, only the main streets in big cities were paved. Cars were scarce, and most people got from place to place by walking or taking a bus. Today Nicaragua has more cars and more paved streets, but horse-drawn cabs and dirt roads are still common. Public transportation is fairly cheap, but it is slow and overcrowded. Car ownership is much more common now than in the past. The majority of car owners live in the largest cities, where most roads are paved. Drivers face hazards, though, such as potholes in the roads, plus a mix of slow-moving traffic that includes pedestrians, bicycles, and horse carts.

Finding your way around can be tricky. Neighborhoods have names but most streets do not, so asking for directions does not help much. Also, Nicaraguans say, "Go toward the lake" or "Go up" instead of "Head south" or "Go left." While other Nicaraguans usually understand because they know where "the lake" is, these directions often seem vague and confusing to foreigners.

Nicaraguans usually live close to their relatives. It is not unusual for several families living in the same neighborhood to be related. Living close together means they do not have to go far to borrow a cup of sugar or find someone to help carry a heavy load. People help each other out all the time by lending food, giving advice, and doing favors. For families living farther apart, the occasional phone call keeps them in touch.

Horse-drawn carts make a pretty sight and are a tourist attraction in Granada.

URBAN PROBLEMS

As Nicaraguan cities continue to grow, urban problems caused by a lack of employment and necessities become harder to control. Poverty and crime go together, especially in cities, and Nicaragua has plenty of both. Alcoholism and drug violence account for an increasing percentage of the crime rate in the country.

Crime and random violence are also on the rise. Violent crime in Managua and other cities is also increasing, and street crimes, such as pickpocketing, are common. Worried about muggings, residents are careful about where they go at night. Occasional armed robberies and even murders occur on crowded buses, at bus stops, and in open markets, particularly the large Mercado Oriental. Gang activity is starting to get a foothold in Managua, although gang violence is much lower than in neighboring countries.

Car theft is another concern. Even if drivers lock their doors, thieves will sometimes take valuable parts, such as mirrors, spare tires, and hubcaps, from unattended vehicles. All public parking lots, such as at supermarkets or restaurants, are attended by guards who keep an eye on cars while their owners are shopping. At some smaller businesses, children earn a little money by charging a small fee to watch a car until the owner returns.

Although the crime rate is increasing, Nicaragua has a crime rate lower than the other Central American countries.

FAMILIES

The average family has four or five children, and poor rural families often have seven or eight. Households usually include uncles, aunts, cousins, or grandparents. Often, with three or four generations living in the same house, children are indulged as well as disciplined. Parents typically believe that spanking or beating their children with a belt is an acceptable form of punishment, but mothers and grandmothers are also generous with praise, hugs, and other gestures of affection.

Nicaraguans place a great deal of importance on maintaining close family relationships. Many couples, especially in rural areas, live together

A family in Granada gathers outdoors to relax.

and raise families without getting a marriage license (which costs money and requires travel to a city). This arrangement is called a common-law marriage. However, most people in the cities, women especially, see the benefits of a legal marriage, which allows them equal rights to their children and the family's possessions.

Nicaraguans often marry young, some as early as thirteen. Almost 40 percent of girls ages fifteen to nineteen are married, and most become mothers at a young age. Teenagers account for nearly 25 percent of all births in Nicaragua, the highest percentage in Central America. Unwed motherhood is also very common. A contributing factor is that abortion is illegal in Nicaragua under any circumstance, including rape or incest. Meanwhile, between a quarter and a third of all Nicaraguan children are chronically malnourished.

GENDER DIFFERENCES Boys and girls are treated differently from a young age. Boys are teased and taunted to teach them to be tough, while girls are doted on and treated more gently. When little boys pick up vulgar language, adults are generally amused by it and only punish them if they direct obscenities at adults. Girls, on the other hand, are punished swiftly if they swear. Boys as young as two are given small jobs or errands to do, such as going to a neighbor's house to buy ice, but girls are not encouraged to be independent. Teenage girls must obey strict rules about going out with friends, while boys are allowed to roam the neighborhood even after dusk.

DOUBLE INCOMES Most Nicaraguan families need at least two incomes just to buy enough food. Because it is hard to find a high-paying job, many adults take on two or three odd jobs to supplement the household income.

Mothers may work part-time in an office, take in neighbors' laundry, and make candy or tortillas to sell on the street. Sometimes, the father or oldest son leaves home to work in Costa Rica or the United States.

Children as young as five or six often help out on the family farm or work as street vendors. In poor families, the children must contribute in one way or another just so everyone has enough food. Wealthy families, on the other hand, often have several maids to cook, clean, and take care of the children.

A boy carries a basket of bananas to help his father in Managua.

WOMEN AND MEN

Although Nicaragua has had a woman president, the country has a long history of male supremacy. Women only received the right to vote in 1955, and today, they are still fighting for equality in a country where being female usually means being a second-class citizen. On the other hand, girls and women in Nicaragua have gradually been gaining more independence compared to their counterparts in some other Latin American countries, thanks in part to the continuing Sandinista influence.

Until the revolution, women had fewer rights and opportunities than men, but that did not keep them from joining the fight to overthrow Somoza. Three out of ten Sandinista soldiers were female. The Sandinista government recognized the important role women played in the revolution and vowed to bring about equality between the genders. One of the first actions of the ruling junta was the passage of an equal-rights law.

Unfortunately, laws cannot change certain facts of Nicaraguan life that make women's lives difficult. Spanish culture has a long tradition of machismo, an attitude of superiority over women that is shared by most men in Nicaragua.

MACHISMO

Machismo defines the power structure between women and men. To Nicaraguans, being masculine means being aggressive, while women's roles are associated with being passive. Men love and honor their mothers very much but do not treat their wives or girlfriends the same way. They can be disrespectful and even abusive toward women. Because household chores and child care are considered women's work, most men refuse to do them.

Other behaviors, such as excessive drinking and getting into fights, are blamed on machismo. Many men think cheating on their wives is permissible because it is in the masculine nature, but this irresponsible conduct causes all kinds of problems. Women in several different households may have children fathered by the same man, and often the father does not support any of them.

The authorities know that some men beat their wives, but unless a woman reports her husband's violence, the authorities cannot do anything to help. The cultural trait of machismo is so ingrained that some women believe they are inferior to men and see the violence against them as inevitable rather than a wrong.

Some mothers today are raising their sons to help out around the house and treat women with kindness and respect, but often boys are confused because they still see their fathers acting according to machismo. Since the revolution, however, the idea of what makes a "good" man has slowly begun to change.

At a rally against violence to women, these signs read "Machismo Kills."

Now, people are defining a good man as one who is responsible toward his family, works hard, and studies to improve himself and his country.

HEALTH

Improved health care was a top priority for the Sandinistas. At the end of the Somoza era, malnutrition was widespread, and water and sanitation systems were grossly inadequate. Pneumonia, tetanus, and measles accounted for more than 10 percent of all deaths, most of them in children under five. Malaria and tuberculosis were common. Within a few years of the Sandinista takeover, the health of the nation had improved and infant mortality had decreased. The Contra War dramatically

reversed that trend, however, and the nation fell into deeper poverty. The devastation caused by Hurricane Mitch in 1998 only exacerbated the already dangerous situation.

Since that time, numerous international health organizations, with the cooperation of the Ortega administration, have worked hard to improve Nicaragua's health care. Access to clean water and sanitation facilities has improved dramatically, though rural areas lag behind urban areas in this and most other health-related categories. Immunizations are now almost universal. The infant mortality rate fell from fifty in 1990 to twenty-one in 2012. The infant mortality rate is the estimated number of deaths per thousand of children under the age of one. This number is often used as an indicator to measure the health and well-being of a nation because factors affecting the health of entire populations can also impact the mortality rate of infants. Nevertheless, severe health challenges remain, mainly caused by insufficient funding.

Aura Nidia Espinosa, 17, (*in yellow shirt*) serves her community in León Province as a *brigadista*, or volunteer health worker. She was trained by the Save the Children organization.

FICTIVE KIN AND GODPARENTS

Children in Nicaragua will probably know someone they call "aunt" or "uncle" who is not really related to them but is a close friend of their parents. This kind of relationship, called fictive kinship, is common in Nicaragua. The tradition of compadrazgo *(kahm-pah-DRAHZ-goh), or coparenting, is another way that Nicaraguans use to expand their families and make sure their children are well taken care of. When a child is born, the parents choose a godmother and a godfather, who become part of the family network. They are expected to assist with the child's moral and religious upbringing, as well as his or her material needs. If the real parents should die, the godparents will take responsibility for the child. Godparents are a source of emotional as well as financial and material support. The two families often exchange favors, advice, food, and clothing, and provide child care support.*

People might ask neighbors, friends, relatives, or coworkers to be their children's godparents, and a lot of thought goes into that decision. Ideally they want to choose someone with whom their child will develop a lasting bond, but other considerations are also involved. Parents think about all these things when selecting godparents for each child in the family. They choose neighbors because they can be easily called on for favors; relatives or friends with a lot of money because they can give their godchildren a financial advantage; doctors because if the child or anyone else in the family gets sick, the doctor would be able to help; relatives in the United States because they might send US dollars or items that cannot be bought in Nicaragua; and members of the father's family, so that if the father is irresponsible, the child will still get support from the godparent.

Access to doctors and hospitals in Nicaragua reflects the basic structure of society. Wealthy and middle-class Nicaraguans can afford good, expensive, and private health care. The poor, however, depend on cheaper public hospitals, which have old equipment and poorly trained doctors. Rural areas often have no health care at all, and poor residents have to travel to the nearest city to see a doctor. Managua contains one-fifth of the country's population, but around half of the available health personnel. Most people in the country do not have a car, so getting to the city to visit a clinic or a specialist when they are sick is an expensive ordeal.

EDUCATION

Before the revolution, few children went to school and over half of the population could not read or write. Many rural areas had no school. The Somoza regime kept the people ignorant so that the people would be powerless to effect change. When the Sandinistas took over, they made education a top priority. They built hundreds of schools and launched a teaching campaign that brought literacy rates up. School was free and compulsory for children from six to thirteen years old, and two five-hour sessions were held each day to accommodate them all. Desks were in short supply, and some students carried theirs to and from school so they would not get stolen overnight. Students were expected to help clean up around the school. Younger ones picked up litter and washed lunch tables, while older children shoveled mud to release stagnant pools of water, the breeding ground of disease-carrying mosquitoes.

A teenage girl does schoolwork in a classroom in Santa Ana de Malacos.

Unfortunately, the Contras worked just as hard to destroy these efforts. By the end of the Contra War, 411 teachers had been killed. The guerrillas also kidnapped sixty-six teachers and fifty-nine students, destroyed forty-six schools, damaged another twenty-one, and forced the temporary closure of more than 550.

After the Sandinistas left the government, public education suffered. When Daniel Ortega became president again in 2007, he launched some official efforts to combat low school attendance and poor student performance. There has been some improvement, but problems remain. Both elementary and high school education are now mandatory and free. However, even "free" public schools charge for textbooks as well as a small monthly fee. Many require simple uniforms, but even this is beyond the budget of many families. School often lasts only a couple of hours a day. In

THE LITERACY CRUSADE

Perhaps the biggest achievement of the Sandinistas was their success in educating Nicaraguans. As soon as Somoza was defeated, the Sandinistas set up adult education programs and vocational and technical training centers. However, their pet project was the Literacy Crusade.

Organizers of the Literacy Crusade called upon everyone over twelve years old who had completed elementary education to help teach reading and writing to thousands of illiterate Nicaraguans. Schools were closed to prepare the young volunteers, called brigadistas (bree-gah-DEEZ-tahs), for the monumental task. In April 1980, after extensive physical, mental, and emotional training, around 80,000 brigadistas were ready.

About 55,000 volunteers went off to the mountains and other rural places to teach the campesinos (kahm-peh-SEE-nohs), or peasant farmers. The rest taught in the cities. In about five months, over 406,000 Nicaraguans learned to read and write.

Because most of the children who volunteered had never experienced life outside the city, the effort became a kind of cultural exchange. Brigadistas carried backpacks full of everything they might need. They were sent to homes that were generally several miles apart, and each taught a family or two. The city children were often surprised to find that campesinos did not know what a television or a car was. In addition to teaching, brigadistas were expected to participate in the family's farmwork and household chores. Many later reported that the experience was the most inspiring thing they had ever done.

Today the literacy campaign continues. In 2015, the literacy rate in Nicaragua was 82.8 percent. The target is to bring the illiteracy rate below 5 percent (or a literacy rate of 95 percent)– the threshold set by the United Nations Educational, Scientific and Cultural Organisation (UNESCO) to declare a country free of illiteracy.

very remote areas, where schools may be inaccessible to some families, it's still customary for children to work for their parents from a young age and enforcing school attendance is difficult.

Though secondary school is mandatory, most children complete primary school only, if that. The main obstacle to fixing the schools is poverty. Critics say Ortega's government is not providing enough funds to fix the problems in the education system. Nicaragua has the smallest annual budget in Central America, and the smallest budget for education. In 2010, the government expenditure on education was 4.4 percent of GDP, which was a significant improvement over previous years. Teacher pay is also a huge concern. Nicaraguan teachers are the poorest paid teachers in Central America, and even in Nicaragua they are among the poorest paid of all professions.

Although the statistics are slowly improving, there remains a large gap between the government's goals and reality in Nicaragua today.

The school year in Nicaragua runs from February through November.

INTERNET LINKS

www.ipsnews.net/2009/04/nicaragua-literacy-campaign-changing-womenrsquos-lives
From the Inter Press Service, this is an interesting article about the literacy campaign

nicaraguadispatch.com/2012/07/childhood-pregnancies-on-the-rise
This is a report on teen pregnancy in Nicaragua.

www.ticotimes.net/2013/02/01/is-nicaragua-s-education-system-failing
This report on the Nicaraguan education system explains some of the problems.

www.unicef.org/infobycountry/nicaragua_statistics.html#125
UNICEF's list of basic statistics for Nicaragua includes health and education indicators.

RELIGION

Originally built in 1534, La Merced Church in Granada has been destroyed and rebuilt twice over its long history.

RELIGIOUS FREEDOM AND RELIGIOUS tolerance are guaranteed by the Nicaraguan Constitution and promoted by the government. The country has no official religion, but the most widely practiced faith is Roman Catholicism. However, Catholicism has declined in recent years, which is the trend throughout Latin America. In the 1960s, over 95 percent of Nicaraguans belonged to the Catholic Church. In 2013, that figure decreased to 47 percent. Protestants make up around 37 percent of the population, and another 12 percent claim no religion.

8

Fifty percent of Nicaraguan Protestants say they were raised Catholic.

ROMAN CATHOLICISM

Ever since the Spanish brought Roman Catholicism to Nicaragua, the Church has played a significant role in Nicaraguan life. Until 1939, Roman Catholicism was Nicaragua's official faith. When the Sandinistas overthrew Somoza Debayle, they unraveled the tight knot between the government and religion. Some factions of the Church supported the Sandinistas, while others aided the Contras. Many of the reforms

Girls receive their First Communion at the Metropolitan Cathedral in Managua in 2012.

the Sandinistas made were too radical for the conservative bishops in Nicaragua. Overall, the church hierarchy resisted change and questioned the government's authority.

LIBERATION THEOLOGY

During the Sandinista revolution, a new concept in religion, called liberation theology, emerged in Nicaragua and other parts of Latin America. Liberation theology teaches that God does not want people to be poor and encourages people to try to change their lives. In the late 1960s, Roman Catholic priests from all over Latin America met in Colombia to discuss liberation theology. Until that time, most Roman Catholics believed poverty and injustice existed because God created them. Poor people assumed their fate was God's will and nothing they did could change it.

The priests who believed in liberation theology taught the poor to take an active role in changing their lives to break free from the cycle of poverty. This progressive movement became known as the Popular Church. Two of its early members were the poet-priest Ernesto Cardenal, who became the minister of culture during the Sandinista regime, and his brother Fernando, who became minister of education and headed the 1980 Literacy Crusade. Priests of the Popular Church made their church services more appealing to the common people by saying Mass in Spanish and by discussing solutions to common problems. Roman Catholic Church leaders opposed the Popular Church movement because they believed people should obey authority and accept their station in life as God's will.

During the Sandinista regime, the Catholic Church forced priests who held government positions to either resign from them or give up the priesthood. They also transferred priests who supported the revolution out of poor barrios and into middle-class neighborhoods, where the people were less likely to support their progressive ideas.

RELIGIOUS FREEDOM

The Sandinistas guaranteed religious freedom, and they tried to include the Catholic Church in the country's reconstruction. However, the Vatican objected to the progressive reforms implemented by the Sandinista regime, and Nicaragua became one of the key places where the Church fought against liberation theology.

The link between religion and politics was especially controversial during the Sandinista years. Many priests were also members of the FSLN, and conservative Catholics opposed this idea, saying that the interests of the Church and the state were in conflict. While the Church and the Sandinistas disagreed on many things, both groups understood the benefits of maintaining a working relationship.

In 1986, President Daniel Ortega held talks with the highest church official, Cardinal Obando y Bravo. The Sandinistas thought if they had Cardinal Obando on their side, the public would also support their efforts. Obando was, and remains, widely respected in Nicaragua. In 2007, he was appointed head of the Peace and Reconciliation Commission, formed to improve relations between the government and church leaders.

In recent years, President Ortega's own Catholicism appears to have deepened and has affected his politics. He credits his wife, Rosario Murilla, a Catholic he married in 2005, with his religious epiphany. Skeptics believe his faith is opportunistic, a political ploy to stay in power. Whatever his motivation, Ortega has embraced a very conservative approach to social issues, such as reproductive rights, that reflects the church's own positions.

PROTESTANT CHURCHES

About 37 percent of Nicaraguans are Protestant or Evangelical. These churches have gained an especially strong footing on the Caribbean Coast. While the Catholic Church is the only religious organization with a strong presence throughout the country, around 118 different non-Catholic faiths are also practiced. Most Nicaraguans who changed their religion did so in the 1970s. They were unhappy that the Catholic Church in Nicaragua had strongly supported the Somoza regime. As the revolution began to build, the poor started to reject Catholicism. The largest Evangelical congregation, the Moravian, has many non-mestizo members from the Mosquito Coast.

The Moravian Church, originally from Germany, was the first Protestant group to gain a foothold in historically Catholic Nicaragua. The Moravians sent missionaries to Bluefields in 1849, and today they are a very important religious influence across the country's Atlantic Coast. In the early 1900s, inter-denominational groups from the United States began to send missionaries to Nicaragua.

In the 1970s some Nicaraguans came to believe that the Catholic Church, which had been introduced by Spanish conquerors, was ignoring the plight of Nicaragua's poor. They felt it was more concerned with supporting whichever government was in power. Numerous Nicaraguans gradually turned toward Protestant denominations. During the 1970s and 1980s, hundreds of thousands left the Catholic Church. When foreign missionaries began to turn leadership over to Nicaraguans, especially in the 1990s, even more people converted to Protestantism.

Up to 85 percent of the Protestant churches in Nicaragua are Pentecostal. Pentecostals are Christians who believe that God's spirit can enter them and help them heal sick people or even make them speak a language they do not know. In many poor, urban neighborhoods, Pentecostals make up more than 50 percent of the population. Assemblies of God is the largest Pentacostal church. Baptist, Seventh-Day Adventist, and non-denominational churches are also important in some areas. These Protestant churches are very small and completely independent, unlike Catholic churches, which are all under the same leadership.

INDIGENOUS BELIEFS

The religion of the Nicarao people was similar to that of the Aztecs. They worshiped corn and natural phenomena, such as the sun and rain, and believed in several gods associated with these elements. When they died, their possessions were buried with them because they believed in reincarnation and thought they would need their belongings in the next life. Other indigenous groups also practiced shamanism, a form of magic. A shaman was believed to have special god-given powers to heal the sick.

In some villages in eastern Nicaragua, shamans still practice traditional healing and are treated with great respect. Many indigenous peoples still go to shamans to worship their ancestors or to communicate with them. Although most indigenous religions have now disappeared, a few vestiges of their traditions remain. Some celebrations, such as the Dance of the Little Devils in Granada, combine Spanish beliefs and indigenous traditional dances and music. Religious holidays, such as the Fiesta of Saint Jerónimo in Masaya, are accompanied by imagery from the old religions.

A white church gleams in the sunlight in Laguna de Perlas (Pearl Lagoon) on the eastern coast of Nicaragua.

FOLK BELIEFS AND SUPERSTITION

Only a few of the original indigenous beliefs remain, but superstitions and folk beliefs are common throughout the country. While educated, urban Nicaraguans have few superstitions, certain interesting notions are common in the countryside and among the poor due to Nicaragua's long tradition of rural folk culture. Many mestizos who live in western Nicaragua believe that blacks along the East Coast practice witchcraft. While black magic and the evil eye are associated almost exclusively with people living on the "other" side, some Nicaraguan men believe all women have the power to cast spells over them. Women are said to know how to enchant and bewitch men into loving them, although few men, if any, have witnessed such a spell being cast.

The tradition seems to be perpetuated by its own built-in factor of secrecy. Women never admit to knowing witchcraft but do not deny it either. Men think mothers teach their daughters how to cast spells and forbid them

NOTABLE CHURCHES

The city of Granada is the best place in Nicaragua to see beautiful churches. Besides the splendid cathedral, three other old churches are located here: the Chapel of Maria Auxiliadora, La Merced, and Jalteva. León is the home of an enormous cathedral—one which was intended for Lima and mistakenly built in León—elaborately decorated with many fine statues in ivory, bronze, and silver. The tomb of Rubén Darío, Nicaragua's most famous poet, is also located here.

The oldest church in Nicaragua, the parish church of Subtiava, is located in León.

The cathedral in Subtiava has a unique feature: a bright yellow sun with a smiling face is painted on the ceiling. When the Spaniards built the cathedral, they included this feature because they thought this would encourage the indigenous people to come to church, as they worshiped a sun god. The Spanish priests hoped to convert the indigenous people to Christianity once they were in the church.

The Granada Cathedral is a colorful landmark.

from ever telling the men about it. In this way, the men are kept wondering if witchcraft exists. The most common spell is the cigar spell. If a woman wants to make her wandering husband come back to her, she should chant a certain incantation over the smoke of a cigar that she must light at midnight.

Other stories and legends from the western region indicate belief in ghosts, devils, and evil spirits. Some people believe that when a mother dies, her soul remains on Earth to watch over her children. Her spirit is said to roam the land of the living until all her children have grown old and passed on. The story of La Cegua (also spelled La Segua), an enchanted woman who roams at night and makes a low whistling sound, is often associated with curses and spells. In some versions, she has the face of a horse. Nicaraguans believe that anyone who sees Cegua might have a change of luck, usually for the worse. Another popular story tells of people who can change humans into animals because they have sold their souls to the devil. Possession by the devil is usually thought to cause insanity or make people cruel and evil.

In eastern coastal communities, folklore is more likely to involve nature and animals. A Miskito legend explains the seasons by personifying summer and winter as two people arguing over whether sun or rain is better for the land. Winter suggests they take turns demonstrating their powers to decide. Summer makes everything too hot and dry, killing plants, animals, and people. Winter creates rain, then has to stop for a while to let the rain dry up. In the end, the seasons decide to take turns working and resting so there will be a correct balance of rain and heat.

An actor dresses as La Cegua in the traditional celebration called Los Agüizotes, in Masaya, Nicaragua. The festival, which takes place on the last Friday of October, celebrates the myths and legends of Nicaragua.

INTERNET LINKS

www.nicaragua.com/culture/folklore
More information about Nicaraguan folklore can be found here.

www.nicaragua-community.com/la-cegua
This short article explains some of the legends of the Cegua.

nicaraguadispatch.com/2014/05/what-can-nicaraguans-learn-from-church-state-powwow
"Nicaragua's Catholic Bishops Criticize Ortega Government" examines the relationship between Daniel Ortega and the Catholic Church.

vianica.com/go/specials/27-managua-nicaragua-patron-saint-dominic-festivities.html
This article describes the importance of patron saints and their celebrations.

LANGUAGE

A man reads a newspaper in Estelí, the third-largest city in Nicaragua.

9

NICARAGUANS LOVE TO TALK, AND IT seems they always have something to say. The official language is Spanish, but a few indigenous languages have survived among the Miskitos, Ramas, and Sumos living along the eastern coast. Western aboriginal languages have all but disappeared, but their influence is still seen in place names and nouns in Nicaraguan Spanish. Many streets, schools, buildings, and neighborhoods are also named after famous Nicaraguans, especially revolutionary heroes and martyrs. The dialect of Spanish spoken in Nicaragua is characterized by interesting expressions, unique pronunciations, and the inclusion of indigenous and English words.

If Eskimos have a hundred words for snow, Nicaraguans have a hundred words related to the machete. (A machete is a long knifelike blade used for cutting heavy vegetation.) One word, *machetazo* (mah-sheh-TAH-zoh), describes someone who gets cut by someone wielding a machete. (Ouch.)

NICARAGUAN SPANISH

The language Nicaraguans speak today is a blend of Spanish, indigenous, and Nicaraguan words. The various indigenous groups spoke many

A schoolgirl copies an English lesson from a board in her classroom in Las Camelias, near Granada.

different languages. Most of these became obsolete after the Spaniards arrived and taught their language to the indigenous people. Miskito and other indigenous languages were combined with Spanish, but eventually most people spoke Spanish.

When the Spaniards encountered things for which their language had no words, they adapted the indigenous names but often pronounced them in a slightly different way. That is one reason why Nicaraguan Spanish is a little different from the Spanish spoken in Spain and other Latin American countries. Also, most urban Nicaraguans include some English words and expressions that they picked up from North American music or movies. For example, young Nicaraguans say "I love you" in English, and the popular words for money are the English "money" and "cash."

PRONUNCIATION

Nicaraguans speak informally, often ignoring grammar rules and shortening words or phrases. They almost always drop the *s* sound from the end of words pronounced with an *s* by people in Spain. The often-used expression "va pues," pronounced "bah PWAY," is one example. The term does not really mean anything: it is like saying "All right, then." Nicas say it all the time. When they momentarily have nothing to say, they say, "Sí pues" (see PWAY), or "Yes, then."

POLITICAL SLOGANS

During the Sandinista revolution, several political slogans became popular. The most common, *Patria Libre o Morir* (PAT-ree-ah LEE-breh oh mo-REEHR), or "A Free Country or Death," was originally the motto of General Sandino in his fight against the US Marines. Later it was adopted by the FSLN in its fight to overthrow Somoza. Another Sandinista slogan is *Poder Popular* (poh-DEHR pahp-yoo-LAHR), meaning "Power to the People."

Since Spanish is spoken across Latin America, there are few terms that are unique to Nicaragua. Below are some words that are characteristic of casual Nicaraguan Spanish.

English	Nicaraguan	Pronunciation
What's going on?/What's up?	*ideay*	*eee-dee-EYE*
to embarrass someone	*achantar*	*ah-CHAN-tahr*
awful	*chocho*	*CHOH-choh*
leave a place/go straight/go on a trip	*va de viaje*	*vah deh vee-AH-hey*
boy/girl	*chavalo/chavala*	*cha-BAL-oh/cha-BAL-ah*

Occasionally the Sandinista army would chant *Muerte al Imperialismo Yanqui* (MWAIR-tay ahl im-pair-ee-yah-LEES-moh YAIN-kee), which means "Death to Yankee Imperialism."

People who left the country during the revolution were called *vende patria* (BEHN-day PAT-ree-ah), or country sellers, and the rich were distastefully referred to as *burgués* (bohr-ZHESS), which comes from the French word *bourgeoisie*.

EXPRESSIONS

Nicaraguan Spanish is full of expressions and idioms. "Walking with the avocados" describes someone who has his or her head in the clouds. Someone who brags a lot is said to think he or she is "Tarzan's mother." Someone stupid and irritating is called *baboso* (bah-BOH-soh), which means something like "slimy slug" in English. When people are disgusted, they might exclaim, *"¡Qué barbaridad!"* (KEH bar-bar-ee-DAHD); "how barbaric."

Two very common expressions used during the difficult and shortage-plagued 1980s were *no hay* (noh-EYE), which means "there is none", and *la vida es dura* (lah BEE-dah ehs DOO-rah), which means "life is hard."

The term búfalo (BOO-fah-loh), or "buffalo" describes someone or something strong and robust. If Nicaraguans say someone has a good coconut, it means he or she is smart, and a dunce is called a *burro* (BOO-roh), or "donkey." Someone who cannot make up his or her mind is called *gallo-gallina* (GUY-oh-gah-YEE-nah), or "rooster-hen." Children are affectionately referred to as *monos*, or "monkeys."

There are several proverbs that express the idea that everyone has a bout of bad luck once in a while. One such proverb is "Even the best monkey occasionally drops a zapote." (A zapote is a tropical fruit.)

NAMES AND TITLES

It is a custom to address people older than one with the respectful title *Don* (DAHN) or *Doña* (DAH-nyah). These words derive from the archaic Spanish words for lord and lady. They are formal titles like sir and madam, but they could also be interpreted as Mr. and Mrs. Traditionally, *Don* and *Doña* were also used when speaking to people of a higher social class, and such people were not obliged to return the courtesy. After the revolution, people started to use more informal terms.

Managua residents read newspapers as they wait to vote in the 2006 elections.

Many people also address someone who has published poetry with the title *poeta* (poh-EH-tah). While it is not a formal title, Nicaraguans often use it because they like to treat poets with respect.

In Nicaragua, English first names are common. Spanish names can be tricky to understand because there are different formulas for men's and women's names. Men put their mother's family name at the end of their names, while women drop their mother's name when they get married and add their husband's.

For example, former president Ortega's full name is Daniel Ortega Saavedra—his first name is Daniel, his father's name is Ortega, and his mother's maiden name is Saavedra. An example of a married woman's name is Violeta Barrios de Chamorro. Her first name is Violeta, her father's family name is Barrios, and when she married Pedro Joaquín Chamorro Cardenal, she added his father's family name to the end of her own, prefaced by the small word *de*. Violeta's mother's name is no longer part of Violeta's name.

LOCAL DIALECTS

Early indigenous people communicated by writing hieroglyphics, or symbols that conveyed messages or stories, on special paper made from tree bark.

The native languages of the indigenous groups in eastern Nicaragua shared the linguistic pattern of the Chibcha group of northern South American Natives. Indigenous people in the west, such as the Nicarao, spoke languages derived from the Nahuatl linguistic family. Nahuatl languages include those of the Maya and Aztecs, and other Mexican and southern North American indigenous groups. Indigenous groups in western Nicaragua found it necessary and practical to speak Spanish, giving up their native tongues. By the mid-nineteenth century, only a few people still spoke indigenous languages there.

On the eastern coast, some indigenous people still speak their native languages. The main dialect is Miskito, and some of its words are English. Since the Miskitos have no words for numbers over ten, for instance, they use the English words. They also have a custom of naming their children after whatever they see around them at the time of birth. There is supposedly a man living in Zelaya whose name is General Electric. Some Miskito words are *tingki-pali*, or "thank you very much," and *nakis-ma*, which means "how are you?" English is the primary language of most people of African origin in the region, but Creole—a mixture of English, Spanish, aboriginal, and black Carib languages—is also quite common.

INTERNET LINKS

www.gringoguide200.com/20-ways-to-speak-like-a-nicaraguan
This fun site has a few Nicaraguan phrases and their meanings.

www.nicaragua-guide.com/common-phrases.html
Another site features a list a common expressions and their meanings

ARTS

Angels surround the beloved Nicaraguan poet Rubén Darío in this memorial in Managua.

10

I N NICARAGUA, IT CAN SEEM AS IF ALL revolutionaries are poets. Or, is it that in Nicaragua, all poets are revolutionaries? To be sure, there is a strong affinity between the country's history and the people's love of poetry. Some say Nicaragua is "the land of poets," though Chileans will argue that the epithet belongs to their country.

Almost everyone in Nicaragua has tried their hand at writing poetry, including President Ortega. Much of the poetry written in the last century reflects the atmosphere of oppression, injustice, and fear that hung over Nicaragua for many decades.

Music and dance are vital to the country's culture as well, but first and foremost, Nicaragua is all about poetry. Each summer since 2005, Granada has been the host of the International Poetry Festival, the largest poetry event in Central America. Famous poets come from around the world—and especially from Central America—to read poetry in public squares. Thousands of people turn out to listen. They also enjoy the festival's concerts, art exhibits, and other carnival-like events.

RUBÉN DARÍO

Nicaragua has produced more poets than any other Latin American country. The most famous is Rubén Darío (1867–1916), leader of the modernist movement that freed traditional Latin American writing

A mural of the poet in Chinandega

from European rules. Darío's vision influenced Nicaraguan writing and all of Latin American literature.

Darío was fond of Walt Whitman, Edgar Allan Poe, and the French Parnassians and symbolists. His poetry was based on ordinary objects, but he used his imagination to elevate common experiences. Much of his early verse described the beauty of the Nicaraguan landscape—the flaming sun, the farms, the pigs, and chickens. Darío's poems often associated artistic and spiritual values with Latin America, and materialism and false values with North America.

In Managua, the performing arts center is named after Darío, and the highest national honor for poetry also bears his name. Metapa, the neighborhood in Matagalpa where he was born in 1867, is now called Ciudad Darío as a symbol of respect. There are several Rubén Darío museums in the country and his likeness is featured on many statues and paintings.

In the past two decades, many women have begun publishing poetry. Before the revolution, most popular poets were men, and their poetry was often political. Much of the poetry written by women takes a different perspective and has more to do with love, nature, and beauty beyond the material world.

THE LITERARY VANGUARD

The Literary Vanguard, established in 1927, was a group of writers inspired by Sandino's determination to drive US Marines out of Nicaragua. The Vanguard's goal was the liberation of Nicaraguan literature from foreign domination, to encourage the growth of native literature.

Joaquín Pasos (1914—1947) was an early member of the Vanguard. His poetry is filled with images of thought and emotion that reflect the character of life in Nicaragua. Another *vanguardista* (bahn-gwar-DEE-tah) was Pablo Antonio Cuadra (1912—2002), a popular author who wrote about everyday life in free verse. He knew Sandino in his youth, and his many poems dealing with political injustice show the strong impression Sandino's ideas left on

One of Nicaragua's biggest literary stars today is Gioconda Belli (b. 1948). She is a poet, writer, and political activist. In her younger days, she was actively involved in the Nicaraguan Revolution. She was the FSLN's international press liaison in 1982 and the director of state communications in 1984.

She married a US journalist and today lives in both Managua and Los Angeles. She broke with the FSLN years ago and has become one of President Daniel Ortega's most vocal critics. She's written six novels, a memoir, six books of poetry, and two children's books, as well as numerous smaller pieces of commentary. Her poetry has been awarded many prizes and her 2003 memoir, The Country Under My Skin: A Memoir of Love and War, *is still hailed as a must-read. The* Los Angeles Times *selected it as one of the best books of the year. Belli infuses her poetry with a woman's point of view, both political and erotic, and has become a passionate voice for women's rights. In 2010 she won the Otra Orilla Hispano-American Prize for her novel,* El Pais de las Mujeres *(A Women's Country).*

him. Cuadra also wrote several delightful and brilliant pieces about nature. A versatile writer, Cuadra wrote a drama in 1937, several years before modern theater came to Nicaragua.

Since the 1940s, another great poet, Ernesto Cardenal (b. 1925), has written poems that are probably the most widely read in the Spanish language today. Cardenal, a Catholic priest and former Sandinista revolutionary, was appointed minister of culture in 1979. His early poems were about his love of women, but his more recent poems speak of the beauty of natural things and the wonders and cruelties of urban life. The short stores of Sergio Ramírez (b. 1942) contain characters living uniquely Nicaraguan lives, such as a baseball player who faces execution as a political prisoner. Ramírez published a novel in 1988, *Castigo divino* ("Divine Justice"), which dramatizes a series

A Sandinista revolutionary poet who ended up in a prominent but very different position from Gioconda Belli is Rosario Murillo (b. 1951). She is the wife of President Daniel Ortega and appears to be a powerful political force in her own right in today's Nicaragua. (Coincidentally, she has the same name as one of the wives of Nicaragua's beloved poet, Rubén Darío.)

The country's first lady is also the chief of communications, meaning she is the voice of the government. These days she is far more visible publicly than her husband, and is said to be a fervent Catholic, socialist, and New Age spiritual leader rolled into one. In fact, many in Nicaragua are wondering if Murillo intends to succeed her husband as the next president. The Somoza dynasty has not been forgotten and most Nicas are wary of a new political dynasty.

of uprisings from 1930 to 1961. It is a carefully woven portrait of the nation's troubles. Other famous writers include poets Santiago Argüello (1872—1940) and Gioconda Belli (b. 1948) and novelist Hernán Robleto (1892—1969), author of *Sangre en el Trópico* (Blood in the Tropics).

THEATER

Theater is an important form of artistic expression in Nicaragua. The National Theater School, a teaching facility, presents performances by students. Another small theater, the Justo Rufino Garay Theater Hall, offers drama by professional troupes from all over Latin America. It is also home to one of Nicaragua's most exciting and adventurous theater companies, the El Grupo de Teatro Justo Rufino Garay. The Rubén Darío National Theater hosts leading international productions.

PAINTING AND SCULPTURE

Some important Nicaraguan artists include the sculptor Genaro Amador Lira and Asilia Guillén, a painter best known for her *Las Isletas*, a beautiful landscape of the islands in Lake Guillén lived for a time at the Solentiname art colony, where she became friends with Ernesto Cardenal, the poet-priest who helped establish the colony. Cardenal brought paint, canvas, and brushes to Solentiname for the first time and encouraged residents to paint what they saw around them. About a dozen talented painters, mostly women, emerged from the colony. Their paintings are primitive and bright. Some have political themes, while others are beautiful landscapes and depictions of the richness of tropical life.

ARTS AND CRAFTS

The tradition of folk art began with the pottery, baskets, and weavings of the indigenous people long before the Spanish arrived. The Nicarao people were known for their skill and imagination in carving jade and other precious and semiprecious stones. The Nicarao traded some of these wares in markets where the standard of exchange was usually cacao. Throughout Mexico and Central America, the indigenous peoples produced a variety of crafts, but only a few artifacts have survived.

Today's arts and crafts are often made by people who learned the ancient methods passed down through the generations. It's still possible to see how the early indigenous people might have used their skills and resources. For example, several indigenous groups practiced loom-weaving using cotton thread colored with natural dyes made from plants and minerals. They used coal to make black dye, blackberry fruits for blue, achiote seeds from the annatto tree for red, and clay for yellow. The hardest color to obtain was purple, which came from an insect living on cactus plants. Today indigenous peoples use synthetic dyes but still weave traditional patterns.

Another craft that has been around for a long time is macramé, a way of knotting strings or ropes to make decorative designs. The hammock was also created by the indigenous people, who used little other furniture.

Ernesto Cardenal (b. 1925) is a poet, a priest, a revolutionary, and a mystic. He may easily be said to be Nicaragua's greatest living treasure, though he is quite controversial. He is a critic of the Ortega administration for one thing, and being a fervent liberation theologist, he was sometimes at odds with the Vatican in the past. (Pope John Paul II stripped him of his right to administer sacraments in 1985.) Of course, he's very old at this writing. "I am a revolutionary," he said at age ninety in 2015. "Revolutionary means that I want to change the world."

The history of censorship by unstable and repressive governments in Nicaragua stunted the growth of artistic expression. When he was appointed minister of culture, Cardenal encouraged people to express themselves and be creative. He also promoted the rediscovery of indigenous arts and traditions. Cardenal wanted to bring art out of the museums, which usually charged admission fees, and display it where everyone could see it regardless of their social status.

Cardenal also believed that people should learn to play music, draw, paint, dance, and write poetry and fiction rather than just listen to or look at art. While he was in charge of the ministry of culture, Cardenal helped establish thirty-two centers for the study and appreciation of popular culture across the country. He founded the primitavist artists' colony of Solentiname on Mancarrón, in the Solentiname Islands in Lake Nicaragua.

Two museums, the National Museum in Managua and the Tenderi Museum of Indian Artifacts in Masaya, maintain significant collections of folk and indigenous art, as well as a few pre-Columbian objects.

Dancing and music are very important parts of folk culture. Street performers can be seen in all the major cities, especially Managua. They dress up in elaborate masks and bright costumes to dance, play music, and entertain audiences with skits or songs.

FOLK MUSIC

While Nicaraguans appreciate many types of music, the traditional sounds of folk music are some of the most appealing. The typical Nicaraguan musical genre is called *Son Nica* (sohn NEE-ca) and usually contains driving rhythms along with good instrumentals. The Ritchie Valens tune "La Bamba"—or the Los Lobos rendition—gives a pretty good idea of what Nicaraguan music sounds like. Along the eastern coast, *costeña* (koh-STEH-nyah) music is very popular. It is a combination of reggae and calypso.

Musicians play marimbas in San Juan del Sur.

Some special instruments are used to produce the unique rhythms and melodies of folk music. The *marimba* (mah-REEM-bah) is like a xylophone, but is made of special wood. It has been around for centuries and is still the most popular instrument in folk music. Other pre-Columbian instruments include *maracas* (mah-RAH-kahs), gourds that are dried so the seeds inside produce a rattling sound. The *chirimia* (chehr-MEE-yah) is a woodwind instrument similar to a clarinet.

INTERNET LINKS

www.nytimes.com/aponline/2014/07/28/world/americas/ap-lt-nicaragua-rosario-murillo.html
"Rosario Murillo: Nicaragua's 'First Comrade'" is an interesting article about the wife of President Daniel Ortega.

www.nytimes.com/2015/01/03/world/americas/science-fuels-writing-and-faith-of-a-nicaraguan-poet-.html?ref=topics&_r=0
This article discusses Ernesto Cardenal at the age of ninety.

www.sampsoniaway.org/blog/2011/05/23/interview-with-nicaraguan-writer-gioconda-belli
This website features a 2011 interview with Gioconda Belli.

LEISURE

A man holds three handmade street baseballs.

11

I N THEIR FREE TIME, NICARAGUANS like to relax and have fun with their friends. Sports events, especially baseball games, always attract crowds of spectators. People do not just like to watch; they also like to play baseball, soccer, and other sports. When the weather is really hot, families often go to the beach to cool off in the water and have a picnic lunch. But perhaps the favorite pastime is lounging at home. Nicaraguans love to talk, tell stories, and reminisce. Sometimes they watch TV, but more often they just sit on the front porch and chat with neighbors.

On July 28, 1991, Nicaraguan Dennis "El Presidente" Martinez, playing for the Montreal Expos, became the first Latin American Major League Baseball player to pitch a perfect game. It is said that on this day, the Contras and the Sandinistas set aside their differences to celebrate the historic moment.

BASEBALL—THE NATIONAL SPORT

In most Latin American countries, soccer and bullfighting are the most popular sports, but in Nicaragua the national sport is *béisbol* (BAYZ-bohl), or baseball. The game was introduced to the country by US Marines in the 1930s, and it soon became more popular than soccer.

More than two hundred teams compete at the local and regional levels, and the best ones play in the national championship games.

A batter takes a swing while playing street baseball in Managua.

Most cities have baseball stadiums where people go to watch their home team play. The largest one, the Dennis Martinez National Stadium, is named for the first Nicaraguan player to make it to Major League Baseball. It is the home stadium of the Indios del Bóer baseball team.

Nicaragua has its own pro baseball league, *La Liga Nicaragüense de Béisbol Profesional (LNBP)* ("Nicaraguan Profession Baseball League"), with four teams: the Indios del Bóer (the Indians), the Tigres del Chinandega (the Tigers), the Gigantes de Rivas (the Giants), and the Fieras del San Fernando (the Beasts).

MAKING THE MAJORS The biggest baseball heroes are Nicaraguans who have made it to the US major leagues: pitcher Dennis "El Presidente" Martinez, pitcher Vincent Padilla, infielder Everth Cabrera, and others. In 2015, there were thirty-one players from Nicaragua currently under contract in the Major and Minor Leagues. Since 2010, forty-six Nicaraguan players had signed with a big league team.

In the spring of 2015, Major League Baseball opened a new Amateur Prospect League at the Jackie Robinson Stadium in Managua. The new league is part of a MLB initiative to promote baseball in Latin America, with an eye toward supplying new MLB talent in the future. It provides scouts and team executives the opportunity to evaluate unsigned prospects in games and in a neutral setting. MLB's first Amateur Prospect League opened in the Dominican Republic in 2012.

OTHER POPULAR SPORTS

After baseball, the next favorite sport is soccer. This game is very popular with Europeans, who probably introduced the sport to Nicaragua in the nineteenth century. Teams for men, women, and children are organized in cities, towns, and villages. Basketball and volleyball are two other common recreational sports, and many cities have established teams for adults who enjoy a little

COCKFIGHTING

A widespread activity throughout Latin America—and certainly in Nicaragua—is cockfighting. This extremely popular form of entertainment is primarily a man's domain—a "gentleman's sport" brought over from Spain. (Today, cockfighting is illegal in Spain.) However, women and children often attend as well, as the tournaments are lively, party-like, social occasions. It's a bloody and brutal spectator sport in which men place bets and drink beer while cheering on their favorite bird. Every small town and hamlet has a cockfighting arena.

In a fight, two roosters are pitted against each other in a battle to the death. The birds have razor-sharp blades attached to the backs of their feet so they can more easily cause injury to their opponent. Men who raise roosters for this purpose are called galleros, *and each has his own bird-training methods for increasing an animal's strength and stamina. However, the birds don't have to be trained to fight; it's an instinct.*

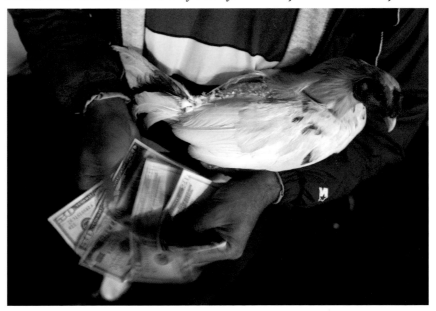

After about fifteen minutes in the ring, both birds are usually quite bloodied. The loser lies dead or dying, and the victor is proclaimed. The losing bird will be made into soup, so the animal is not wasted.

Cockfighting made its way to the United States with Latin American immigrants. US laws ban the blood sport because it is seen as cruelty to animals. The games often continue in secret, however. There is no move to outlaw the practice in Nicaragua; cockfighting is far too beloved a part of the culture.

friendly competition. Junior basketball and volleyball leagues are growing fast because more young people are becoming interested in these sports. Track and field and martial arts are not as common, but are relatively popular. Boxing is quite popular, especially after the success of Managua-born Ricardo "El Matador" Mayorga, who won the World Boxing Association (WBA)/World Boxing Championship (WBC) welterweight title in 2002—2003.

Bullfighting is a traditional Spanish activity that is often part of festivals and celebrations. In Spain, the object of a bullfight is for the matador (the person fighting the bull) to kill the animal, but in Nicaragua the matador has to try to mount and ride the bull. He is judged not only on ability but also on his style.

Nicaraguan amateur boxer Wendy Cruz, 19, trains while her daughter toddles around the gym.

A PLACE TO SOCIALIZE

When they are not playing or watching sports, Nicaraguans enjoy just hanging around with their family and friends. In many neighborhoods, people leave their front door open all day so they can call out greetings to passers-by and invite them in for a cold drink. Most homes have front porches where people gather in the evenings to talk, tell stories, and listen to the radio. When it is really hot, everyone takes a chair out to the porch, faces it inward, and watches television from there. Almost all families have a set of rocking chairs—big ones for adults and little ones for kids. Family time is spent on the porch or in the living room relaxing in their rockers. The chairs can be made of carved wood or woven bamboo.

FAVORITE PASTIMES

Almost every home in Nicaragua has at least one radio. In fact, for every four people, there is one radio. There are more than a hundred radio stations, including two government stations. Nicaraguans listen to music, news, and a variety of political-discussion programs while they do chores around the house and during their free time. In the evenings, some stations broadcast made-for-radio mysteries or soap operas. Many shows from other countries can also be heard on Nicaraguan radio.

There are not as many homes with television sets in Nicaragua as there are in more developed countries, but people who do not own one usually have relatives or neighbors who do. At 7 p.m. on weekdays nearly everyone in the country is seated in front of the television for the *novela* (noh-BEH-lah), or soap opera, which is so widely watched that evening meetings are never scheduled for that hour. In the cities, cable TV is available, and many of the networks that people enjoy in the United States are shown with Spanish dubbing or subtitles. There are also a few nationwide channels that broadcast to anyone with an antenna. Children love to watch cartoons. Other favorites are music videos, talk shows, and old American movies.

Few people can afford to go to the movies often, but when they have a little extra money, films are a big hit. All the major cities have movie theaters that show films, mainly from the United States, in English with Spanish subtitles. Occasionally, a Nicaraguan-made film will appear, usually at one of a few museum theaters.

Internet access is also available, though not widespread. In 2012, about 13.5 percent of the population was online.

A DAY AT THE BEACH

January to April—when the sun beats down hard almost every day and temperatures rise above 100°F (38°C)—is beach season. Nicaraguans head for nearby beaches on weekends and holidays to relax, swim, and have picnics. From Managua, it is an hour-long bus ride to one of several beaches. The most popular ones include Pochomil and Masachapa, located side by side on the Pacific Ocean. One of the most beautiful beaches is El Velero, northwest of Managua. The sea there is great for surfing and swimming, but it costs the equivalent of $6 to enter, so it is more popular with upper-class families and tourists.

Nicaraguan actress Alma Blanco, a star of the film *La Yuma*, is interviewed in Managua in 2010. Blanco won the Best Actress category in four international film festivals for her performance. *La Yuma* was the first movie produced in Nicaragua in twenty years.

A HIDEAWAY IN THE HIGHLANDS

Many middle-class Nicaraguans like to escape to the mountains for relaxing and hiking. One such mountain hideaway is the Selva Negra, a resort and hotel built by third- and fourth-generation German immigrants. The resort owners' German ancestors were traveling across Nicaragua on their way to California during the 1850s when they decided to stay in Nicaragua and grow coffee. (Nicaragua was used by thousands of people as a shortcut to California during the gold rush.)

Selva Negra is known for its sustainable and environmentally friendly method of farming coffee. The owners of the hacienda ("farm") grow coffee in the shade of tall trees as it would have grown in its natural environment. This encourages dozens of species of tropical birds, including the rare three-wattled bellbird, to roost in the trees. Vacationers and tourists can choose from any of fourteen hiking trails and several horseback riding trails that will take them into the forest to see the birds, ferns, wild orchids, and the trees of the cloud forest.

Selva Negra also practices self-sufficiency and recycling. The food served at the resort is cultivated at the hacienda. The vegetables served at the table are grown organically, that is, no chemicals and pesticides are used, and fertilized with waste products from the animals on the hacienda. These animals, which include cattle and fowl, provide meat, dairy products, and eggs.

Although Lake Managua, Lake Nicaragua, and several smaller lakes do not have pretty, sandy beaches, they do offer other interesting activities. Visitors go to the lakes to row or see the volcanoes, but the water is polluted in some places, and swimming is not a good idea. Usually there are playgrounds, ice cream stands, and historical landmarks near the lakes.

Swimmers enjoy the waters of Laguna de Apoyo, the crater lake.

Not far from Lake Managua, at Acahualinca, is Nicaragua's most significant archaeological artifact. In the nineteenth century, ancient footprints were discovered in a patch of dried mud that had been preserved by a thick layer of volcanic rock and ash. The footprints were made more than six thousand years ago by men, women, and animals, including a deer and possibly a jaguar. They head toward the lake; it was initially believed that these people were fleeing an erupting volcano, but that has since been disproved. Instead, tests have shown that they were walking at normal speed and were carrying either a heavy load of supplies or children.

INTERNET LINKS

www.baseball-reference.com/bullpen/Liga_Nicarag%C3%BCense_de_B%C3%A9isbol_Profesional
Baseball-Reference.com devotes a page to an overview of the Nicaraguan Professional Baseball League.

www.selvanegra.com
This is the home site of the Selva Negra nature reserve and coffee estate.

content.time.com/time/world/article/0,8599,1590985,00.html
This *Time* magazine article gives a first-hand look at cockfighting in Nicaragua.

FESTIVALS

A dancer performs at the Joy for Life Carnival in Managua.

12

CULTURALLY, NICARAGUA IS A MIX OF Spanish-European traditions, Roman Catholic rituals, and indigenous customs. These elements play important roles in the nation's festivals and holidays. Throughout the year, Nicaraguans celebrate many holidays with parades, grand fiestas, elaborate meals, and religious ceremonies. Music and dancing make these events particularly enjoyable.

Some holidays are religious, such as Purísima and Easter. Some are anniversaries of historical events. Whatever the cause for celebration, Nicaraguans know how to relax and have a good time.

PURÍSIMA

One of the most important Roman Catholic holidays in Nicaragua is Purísima, also called *La Gritería*, a celebration of the Virgin Mary. In most areas, it is celebrated on December 7, but in Managua the holiday involves a week of festivities.

The tradition of celebrating Purísima originated centuries ago when the Cerro Negro volcano erupted. It spilled lava for days and the people in nearby León feared that it would never stop. Then one day, they placed a statue of the Virgin Mary on the smoldering ground near the volcano and the volcano soon became still. The people believed that the

A nun sings to the image of the Virgin Mary during Purísima.

Virgin Mary had stopped the volcano and saved them from further harm.

Preparations for this holiday begin weeks in advance with several families in each neighborhood setting up elaborate altars to the Virgin Mary. They invite friends and relatives over on the evening of December 6 to see the altars and sing hymns in Mary's honor. The altars are draped in fabric and decorated with lights, candles, flowers, branches, and leaves. Each one features an image of the Virgin Mary. Chairs are set up so visitors can stop and pray at the altar. Often, the host gives each guest a cold drink, a piece of sugarcane, a small gift, and an orange or lime before they leave. Because it can be expensive to set up these displays and host large numbers of guests, people take turns at being host, and those who have altars one year are usually guests at friends' homes the following year.

In Managua, the celebration includes an impressive fireworks display on December 7. A big festival is held in some cities, and crowds gather around professionally built altars to sing. Some families eat big feasts of roast pork and traditional Nicaraguan dishes.

OTHER RELIGIOUS HOLIDAYS

In some cities, like León, Purísima is the biggest holiday, but Christmas and Easter are also celebrated with great joy. On Christmas Eve, families sit down to a special meal of chicken or turkey. Some people attend Christmas Eve Mass, and at midnight almost everyone goes out into the street to exchange *abrazos de paz* (ah-VRAH-soh day PAH), or "hugs of peace," with friends and neighbors. Christmas trees decorated with lights and ornaments are a common sight, as are bare branches covered with cotton. Most homes have some sort of Christmas decoration.

Gift-giving at Christmas is common, but most people have little money to buy presents. Younger children believe in the God Child, a mythical figure who brings gifts. Poor children may not get a gift from their parents or the God Child, but they are almost certain to receive one from their godparents. Even if they cannot afford gifts for their own children, godparents will make sure their godchildren have something to open on Christmas.

Easter, called *Pascua* in Nicaragua, is usually celebrated by attending church and visiting relatives. The week before Pascua is called Semana Santa, or Holy Week. Activities include processions in remembrance of the crucifixion. On Good Friday, people show respect for Jesus's suffering by going to church or praying at home. The rest of the week, however, is considered a good time for vacationing.

The holiday falls at the height of the dry season when it is very hot, so much of the population can be found relaxing and playing at the beach. For sports fans, a popular event is the Nicaraguan baseball play-offs, held annually during Semana Santa.

Children reenact the crucifixion of Jesus on boats that float between the islets of Lake Nicaragua during Holy Week celebrations in 2013.

SAINTS' DAYS

Another occasion for revelry is the day set aside by each town or village for honoring a patron saint. In Managua, the feast of Santo Domingo de Guzman is observed over a period of ten days. From August 1 to August 10, Managuans attend parties, hold parades, and watch bullfights, cockfights, and horse races. The main event is a lively procession as the tiny statue of Saint Dominic is carried from its sanctuary in the southwestern side of town to its temporary home in the old center. The celebration honors Nicaraguans' indigenous heritage as well as their Catholic saint. Church ceremonies commemorate Saint Dominic, but some festival rituals are symbols of the time before the Spanish introduced Catholicism.

PUPPETS WITH A PURPOSE

Crowds of excited children and adults gather around La Gigantona, *or "The Giant Lady," a lavishly decorated, 8-foot-tall (2.4 m tall) puppet dancing in the village square. An indigenous tradition that has been around for hundreds of years,* Las Gigantonas *are seen at political rallies, markets, and festivals in many towns.*

Sometimes La Gigantona is accompanied by "El Enano Cabezon" (the Big-Headed Dwarf). The Giant Lady is the tall, light-skinned, rich Spanish woman and the Dwarf is a short, poor, indigenous or mestizo man who is nevertheless very smart (hence the big head). To the accompaniment of loud drums, the two puppets dance out the struggle between social classes and cultures that represent Nicaragua.

The festivals honoring Saint Jerónimo in Masaya and Saint Sebastian in Diriamba are occasions for folk artists to exhibit their work. Both cities are known for their beautiful indigenous handicrafts. In León, *La Merced* ("Our Lady of Mercy"), is a religious holiday. People celebrate by attending church and marching in a procession carrying a large image of La Merced.

On November 1, Nicaraguans throughout the country honor All Saints' Day by going to church and praying to the various saints. The next day is called All Souls' Day, a time to remember the dead. For a week leading up to this day, people go to cemeteries to clean the graves in preparation for All Souls' Day. They also place flowers on the graves of their loved ones. Often they take something that was special to the dead person, such as a hat, a bottle of the person's favorite drink, or a picture, and leave it on the grave. On the day itself, families take picnic lunches to eat beside their family members' graves. Many spend the day there, visiting other families.

IMPORTANT EVENTS

The oldest national holiday celebrates the day Central American countries became independent from Spain. Independence Day, observed on September 15, brings colorful parades, fireworks, and speeches to the central plaza in most cities. In Granada, this day is celebrated with much fanfare. Schoolchildren and high school drum and bugle corps march through the streets to the plaza, where everyone gathers to listen to speeches by local government officials.

The Sandinista revolution is celebrated on July 19. People from all over Nicaragua take buses to Managua, where a huge rally is held. During the 1980s, the anniversary of the Sandinistas' defeat of Somoza was a popular time for the Sandinista government to speak out about its plans for reform. Today this day has become a time to remember the many people who died during the struggle to defeat Somoza.

Mothers' Day is an important occasion for Nicaraguans. Even people who do not live near their mothers try very hard to visit them on this day. Mothers are sometimes honored by being serenaded early in the morning or at night, after dinner.

INTERNET LINKS

www.nicaragua-community.com/la-gigantona
Here you will read about the tradition of *La Gigantona*, with some history.

vianica.com/go/specials/27-managua-nicaragua-patron-saint-dominic-festivities.html
This website provides a very informative article on patron saint festivities in Managua.

vianica.com/go/specials/8-december-celebrations-nicaragua.html
This website offers an in-depth look at Holy Week traditions.

FOOD

Bags at a market are rolled open to reveal corn, rice, and beans, the staples of the Nicaraguan diet.

13

ORN IS KING IN NICARAGUA. Ground corn, in particular, forms the basis of many dishes and even beverages. Corn was a staple of the indigenous people of Central America in pre-Columbian times and it's a staple of Nicaraguan cuisine today. Like most Latin American food, the cuisine is *criollo*—a fusion of Indian and Spanish tradition based on local ingredients.

Some Nicaraguans, especially some of the indigenous peoples, eat guinea pigs, tapirs, turtle meat and turtle eggs, lizards, armadillos, and boas. The consumption of turtle meat and eggs is a particular concern to the government as sea turtles are endangered.

A clerk shows an iguana to potential buyers at the Oriental Market in Managua.

A woman cooks tortillas at a market in Managua.

Although the cuisine differs in various regions of the country, there are similarities that run through all. The food is not spicy, though it is well seasoned, and corn is important to all. People eat corn tortillas with most meals. Typically, these tortillas are large, thin, and made with white corn.

On the Pacific Coast and in the central regions of the country, meals include beans and rice, beef, chicken, or pork, and local fruits and vegetables. These include jocote, mango, papaya, tamarind, bananas, pipian, and avocado, and roots such as yucca and quequisque. The quequisque is a yam-like tubor that is thinly sliced and fried up like a potato chip. Nicaraguan dishes are often flavored with cilantro, oregano, and achiote. The foods of the Atlantic Coast are heavily influenced by Caribbean cuisine. Cooks here use Afro-Caribbean spices, coconuts, and seafood.

SHOPPING

In any of the western coastal cities of Nicaragua, there is always a supermarket nearby. Imported goods as well as locally produced foods are generally available. Supermarkets also sell cosmetics, clothes, books, stationery, and pots and pans. Shopping for the household is usually a woman's task, although it is also common for mothers to send their children to the market.

For many Nicaraguans, supermarket prices are too high, so they also shop at outdoor markets where vendors sell their goods from individual stalls, and bargaining is common. Many women prefer to shop this way because the produce and meat are fresher than what they can find at a supermarket.

At smaller outdoor markets, vendors walk around with baskets of fruit or other items, and shoppers bargain with vendors over prices until they settle on one that satisfies both parties.

Some markets are held indoors, but the largest ones take up whole blocks of city streets. One of the biggest is the Mercado Oriental in Managua, where vendors are often lined six-deep along sidewalks and streets. Many items found here are black market goods, so they are too expensive for most Nicaraguans. Another important market in Managua is the Mercado Roberto Huembas. At both markets, there are dozens of booths selling staples, such as rice and beans. However, some stalls also sell specialized products—one booth at Huembes sells everything that is needed for cake decorating.

A watermelon vendor watches for customers at his stall in the Oriental Market in Managua.

Shopping for food at local markets is often a daily requirement because food spoils so quickly in the hot climate. Another place where people get fresh food is at local general stores, which are often located in the converted front rooms of people's houses. Locals know where to go even though most of these stores have no signs. These shops carry staple items and homemade goods, such as tortillas. It is common for people who have refrigerators to buy milk in large amounts and sell it to their neighbors each day. The same goes for people who have ovens—they make tortillas to sell to neighbors who do not have ovens.

SHORTAGES AND HIGH PRICES

Food shortages made life difficult for Nicaraguans during the rule of the Sandinista government. As one Nicaraguan lady says, "Now there is food and no money to buy it, but in those days, there was no food available to buy." What little food was available at supermarkets was nearly all imported. The price controls set by the government weakened farmers' incentives and

In 1987, a long line of people wait outside a supermarket for a chance to buy some of the meager supply of meat that is available.

caused a drop in local production. The Contra War also took a huge toll on local production. Many farmers were drafted into the national army, reducing the labor force on farms. In addition, the Contras damaged fields of crops, food storage areas, and trucks transporting food to undermine the Sandinistas' efforts to raise the country's standard of living.

By the late 1980s, many thousands of acres of good farmland were abandoned because they were in the war zone. Government attempts at rationing food or subsidizing its cost were ineffective because production had decreased so much. The price of food increased so drastically that by 1988, even the maximum basic salary for a worker supporting a family of six would only buy about 60 percent of what economists call the basic basket of essential products. Families had to have at least two incomes, and even then it was hard to make ends meet. Shortages persisted after the Chamorro administration began in 1990, but since then increased foreign trade and local production have made food less scarce. Today most supermarkets are fully stocked, but people still cannot afford to buy many necessities. One way Nicaraguans cope with this lack of purchasing power is to supplement their diet with food they can grow themselves.

COOKING

Like shopping, cooking is usually a woman's job. Nicaraguan specialties often are made using cornmeal. The *nacatamale* (nah-caw-ta-MAL-eh) is considered by many to be Nicaragua's national folk food. It consists of a cornmeal tamale filled with pork, rice, potato, onion, tomato, and green pepper. *Atoles* (ah-TOY-ehs) are deep-fried tortillas with cheese and spices inside. The most traditional dish throughout the country is *gallo pinto* (GUY-oh PEEHN-toh), or "painted rooster." It is a mixture of red beans, rice, onions, garlic, and seasonings, all fried in a little oil until crisp. The name comes from the red and white colors of the beans and rice. Most Nicaraguan families eat it at least once a day. Two very common beverages are *refrescos* (ray-FREHS-kohs) and *pinol* (PEEHN-ohl). Refrescos are made of fresh fruit juice with a little sugar and water added. Locals can usually tell what flavor the drink is by looking at its color: mango is light orange, papaya is yellow, and tamarind is brown. Refrescos are sold with crushed ice in a plastic bag tied at the top. People hold the bag in one hand, bite off a corner, and suck the drink out. Pinol is a drink made of toasted ground cornmeal mixed with water or coconut milk and a flavoring like cinnamon or ginger. If it is mixed with some ground cacao, it is called *pinolillo* (peehn-oh-LEE-yoh). These beverages are commonly served in a hollowed-out gourd.

Gallo pinto (here made with black beans) is served here with eggs and tropical fruit.

Fruits and vegetables are frequently eaten raw or used in preparing a meal. Tomatoes, cabbages, sweet potatoes, avocados, and yucca are common choices. Fruits can be used to make a number of juices, jams, and sauces. Nicaraguans make a wide variety of dishes out of bananas, including porridge, milk shakes, and cakes.

MEALS AND ETIQUETTE

Corn, rice, and beans are staples in every Nicaraguan home. Fortunate families usually have cheese, butter, milk, and tortillas to go with their meals, and once a week or so they have a stew or some other special dish. Less fortunate people might eat only rice and beans. A standard breakfast in a working-class home might consist of two slices of bread with butter (if it is available), an orange or a banana, and heavily sugared coffee. Lunch is usually beans and rice, the leftover bread from breakfast, and maybe a piece of cheese, accompanied by

A typical Nicaraguan lunch of pork, beans, plantains, and rice

a fruit drink made from lemons or oranges picked from the backyard and sweetened with lots of sugar. Chicken soup may be served instead of beans and rice. A typical dinner consists of gallo pinto, tortillas, and fried cheese.

A common practice is the sharing of special food items. When someone in the neighborhood prepares a stew, pasta, roasted meat, or other special meal, she is obligated by social norms and customs to share the food with others in the neighborhood. For example, if a neighbor who stops by to chat while you are cooking "helps" by stirring the pot or throwing in a few spices, she should be given a serving when the meal is ready. Also, whoever lends any vegetables, spices, or other ingredients to the cook is assured a sample of the finished product. Nicaraguans believe that you will have bad luck if others see you being stingy, so you have to share with everyone who saw you fixing a special meal—and anyone who even heard you were serving one.

HOLIDAY FEASTS

Meals become an elaborate production during holiday seasons. Women begin shopping and preparing feasts days in advance of Christmas, Easter, and Purísima. Holiday feasts are shared with friends and family, and sometimes the diners can number in the hundreds. Some of the special foods usually reserved for holiday meals are *chicharrón* (chee-chahr-ROHN), or fried pork skins and *vigorón* (bee-gohr-OHN), which is *chicharrón* served on a bed of raw shredded cabbage and cooked sliced yucca. An especially prized dish is *bajo* (BAH-hoh), a hearty beef or pork stew made with many indigenous vegetables and tubers.

A holiday feast would not be complete without sweets. Easter season brings *buñuelos* (boo-nyu-EH-los), fried dough made of cassava, white cheese, and egg, topped with hot sugar syrup. For Christmas, women prepare *almivar* (al-mee-VAHR), a grated candied fruit. Purísma specialties include a crumbly bar made of ground corn, ginger, and sugar, called *alfajor* (al-fa-HOR), plus *ayote en miel* (a-YOT-te en mee-EL), which is squash cooked in honey, and light, crispy *espumillas* (es-pum-EE-yahs) or meringues. Children would go door to door for sweets, such as caramel and chopped sugar cane.

KITCHENS

Aside from the living room, the kitchen is the most often used room in a typical middle- or lower-class home. It is where families eat because small houses do not have separate dining rooms. Women wash clothes and bathe babies in the kitchen sink or in a large wash basin kept outdoors. A radio is almost

Buñuelos are festively presented.

always found in the kitchen because Nicaraguans love to listen to music. Usually the kitchen table is the only table in the house, so children often do their homework there. Upper-class families have dining rooms where meals are usually served. They can also afford to hire maids to cook and clean, and the kitchen then becomes the cook's domain.

Average households might have a refrigerator or a wood stove, but not both. Neighbors often "borrow" each other's kitchens when they need to bake or keep food cold. In the mornings, coffee is brewed, not in an electric coffee maker but in a big pot on the stove. People without stoves cook on two-burner electric hot plates.

A big frying pan is essential, and most kitchens also have several pots in various sizes, enough eating utensils and plates for each family member, as well as a few extra, and a large jug for storing boiled water for drinking. Cups and glasses are scarce, so people often drink out of cut-off soft drink bottles with the edges smoothed. A hollowed-out gourd works like a thermos cup, keeping drinks cold even without ice. Milk and juice are stored in small

Today there are three McDonald's restaurants in Managua. They serve standard McDonald's fare, cooked the standard McDonald's way. But that was not always the case.

In 1975, the franchise opened its doors to Nicaraguans who had never before seen the Golden Arches. The establishment also became popular with foreign visitors who wanted something familiar to eat. However, within a few years, customers began complaining to McDonald's International (the parent company of McDonald's branches) about the quality of food served at McDonald's Managua. In 1986, the owner of the local McDonald's received a letter from headquarters that warned, "Do not sell cheeseburgers unless they contain cheese." Well, that was easier said than done in a country where even milk was in short supply. After the Sandinista revolution, supplies were limited because of the US trade embargo. McDonald's Managua could not import pickles for their Big Macs or the regulation paper to wrap burgers. For a while, the restaurant used Russian wrappers, but customers complained they made the food smell (and taste) like wet cardboard.

The staff used white cheese when there was no yellow cheese, substituted cabbage for lettuce, and when they ran out of french fries, they served deep-fried cassava (a tropical plant with a starchy root that is also used to make tapioca). Coca-Cola was rarely available, so the restaurant sold pitaya *(pee-TAH-yah), a tropical cactus-fruit drink.*

Today, the McDonald's restaurants in Managua sell what they are supposed to—the Pollo McCrispy, the Cuarto de Libra con Queso, and of course, the Big Mac.

plastic bags that hold one or two servings. Fresh orange juice is served in its own natural cup, made by slicing off the top and carefully cutting away the skin. The spongy white part is left intact so one can hold the orange in one hand and eat it by squeezing and sucking.

RESTAURANTS

Although the majority of Nicaraguans do not eat out very often, there are enough wealthy locals and foreigners to keep even the most expensive restaurants in business. Fast food in Nicaragua means one of three things. The first option is eating at an outdoor stand called a *fritanga* (free-TAN-ga), where grilled chicken, beef, and pork are served. The second, much more expensive option, found mainly in Managua, is American fast food chains such as Subway or McDonald's. These chains serve exactly the same food found at their US outlets, and cost the same too, which means it can cost ten times as much to eat at McDonald's as to eat at a *fritanga*. For a third option, Nicaragua has its own American-style fast food. Several chains serve delicious fried chicken and chicken strips, fries, and soft drinks.

A street food vendor cooks a pot of baho (beef with local vegetables, yucca, and banana leaves).

INTERNET LINKS

vianica.com/go/specials/2-nicaraguan_food.html
Vianica's site takes a good look at traditional Nicaraguan foods.

vianica.com/go/specials/14-nicaraguan-fruits.html
The site also has an interesting overview of Nicaragua's tropical fruits.

www.whats4eats.com/central-america/nicaragua-cuisine
This site has several easy-to-follow recipes.

SALPICÓN ("NICARAGUAN MINCED BEEF SALAD")

This beef dish is usually served cold or at room temperature.

2 pounds (907 grams) beef round, cut into 2-inch (5.08-centimeter) cubes

1 large white or yellow onion, peeled and cut into 1 inch pieces

Salt

2 teaspoons (9.9 milliliters) black peppercorns

1 bay leaf

4 medium garlic cloves, peeled and smashed

1 large green bell pepper, cored and seeded

Cold water

1 lime

Place beef, half of onion, 2 teaspoons salt, peppercorns, bay leaf, and garlic in large pot. Add enough cold water to cover ingredients by 2 inches. Bring mixture to boil over medium-high heat, then reduce heat to medium-low and simmer until beef is cooked through, about 15 minutes or until tender.

Drain beef and allow to cool about 10 minutes. Discard onion pieces, peppercorns, bay leaf, and garlic.

Place half of beef, half of remaining bell pepper, and remaining onion in a food processor and pulse until mixture is finely chopped. Alternatively, mince as finely as possible with a knife. Transfer to large mixing bowl and repeat with remaining beef, bell pepper, and onion. Season squeeze lime over beef and toss to combine. Season to taste with salt.

Serve immediately or refrigerate. This salad is usually served over white rice, and with a green salad. Serves 4 to 6.

PASTEL DE TRES LECHES ("THREE MILK CAKE")

This dessert is popular all over Latin America, but is thought to have originated in Nicaragua. The cake is soaked in three kinds of milk.

1½ cups (355 mL) flour

1 tsp (4.9 mL) baking powder

½ cup (1 stick, or 8 tablespoons; 118 mL) unsalted butter, softened

¾ cup (177.4 mL) sugar

5 eggs

1 tsp (4.9 mL) vanilla

2 cups (473 mL) whole milk

2 (14 ounce) cans sweetened condensed milk

1 (10 ounce) can evaporated milk

1½ cups (355 mL) heavy whipping cream

½ cup (118 mL) sugar

1 tsp (4.9 mL) vanilla

Preheat oven to 350°F (175°C). Grease and flour a 9 x 13-inch baking pan. Sift flour and baking powder together and set aside. Cream butter and the ¾ cup sugar together until fluffy. Add eggs and 1 teaspoon vanilla; beat well. Add the flour mixture to the butter mixture a little at a time; mix until well blended. Pour batter into prepared pan. Bake at 350°F (175°C) for 30 minutes. Pierce cake all over with a fork.

Combine the whole milk, condensed milk, and evaporated milk together. Pour over the top of the cooled cake. Refrigerate for at least two hours, or until milk mixture is absorbed.

Whip cream, ½ cup of the sugar, and 1 tsp vanilla together until thick and cream holds soft peaks. Frost the cake with the whipped cream.

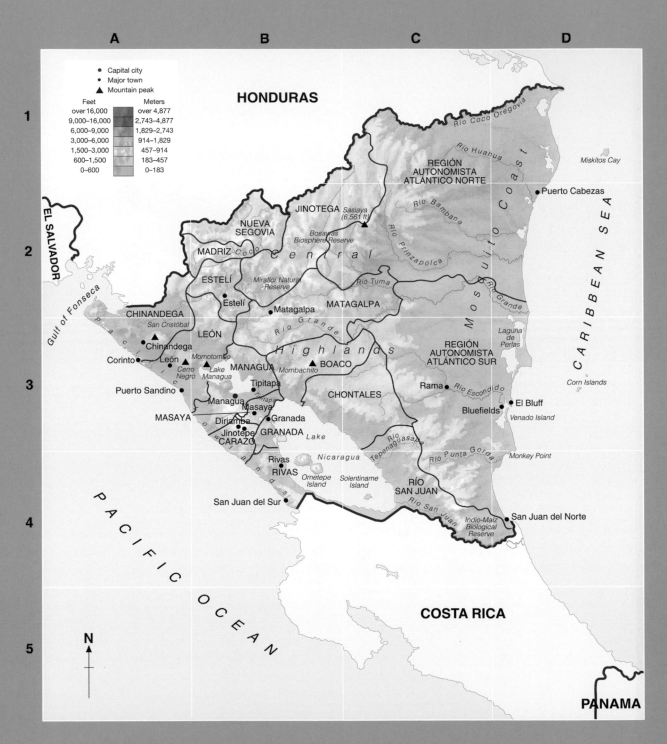

MAP OF NICARAGUA

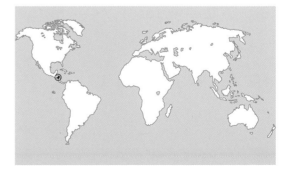

ECONOMIC NICARAGUA

Agriculture

- Bananas
- Cattle
- Coffee
- Corn
- Rice
- Sugarcane
- Vegetables

Natural Resources

- Fishery
- Forestry
- Gold Mine
- Petroleum Refinery

Manufacturing

- Beverage processing
- Food processing
- Textiles

Services

- Airport
- Port
- Tourism

OVERVIEW

Nicaragua's economy is slowly recovering from the disasters that occurred in the 1990s: the drastic fall in coffee prices and the effects of Hurricane Mitch. While the service sector contributes more to the country's GDP, the majority of Nicaragua's workforce are employed in the agricultural sector. Chronic problems, such as unemployment and underemployment, remain unresolved. Nicaragua is also still heavily dependent on foreign aid.

GROSS DOMESTIC PRODUCT (GDP)

US$30.05 million (2014)

CURRENCY

1 córdobaoro (NIO) = 100 centavos
Notes: 100, 50, 20, 10, 5, and 1
Coins: 25, 10, and 5
US$1 = 26 Córdoba (2014)

GDP SECTORS (2014)

Agriculture: 14.9 percent
Industry: 28.8percent
Services: 56.4 percent

LAND AREA

50,336 square miles (130,370 sq km)

LAND USE (2014)

Arable land: 12.5 percent
Permanent crops: 2.5 percent
Other: 85 percent

UNEMPLOYMENT RATE

7.4 percent plus considerable underemployment (2014)

INFLATION RATE

6.1 percent (2014)

AGRICULTURAL PRODUCTS

Coffee, bananas, sugarcane, cotton, rice, corn, tobacco, sesame, soy, beans, beef, veal, pork, poultry, dairy products

INDUSTRIAL PRODUCTS

Food processing, chemicals, machinery and metal products, textiles, clothing, petroleum refining and distribution, beverages, footwear, wood

MAJOR TRADE PARTNERS (IMPORTS)

United States 17.6 percent, 14.7 percent, Costa Rica 9 percent, Mexico 13 percent, Guatemala 8.3 percent, El Salvador 5.6 percent (2013)

MAJOR IMPORTS

Machinery and equipment, raw materials, petroleum products, consumer goods

PORTS AND HARBORS

Bluefields, Corinto, El Bluff, Puerto Cabezas, Puerto Sandino, Rama, San Juan del Sur

CULTURAL NICARAGUA

Coffee
Coffee plantations thrive in Nicaragua's highlands, where the combination of tropical climate and high elevation is just right. Many plantations also offer tourist accommodations, especially around Matagalpa.

Revolutionary Murals
The facade of many of Estelí's buildings are decorated with murals painted by the town's youth. These paintings, numbering over a hundred, depict the history, culture, and daily life of the artists. The town was the site of many battles and bombings during the country's civil wars.

Dugout Canoes
Hand-carved wooden boats are the only form of transportation for many Miskito people living near Puerto Cabezas (also known as Bilwi). The boats are used to travel along the coastal marshes and rivers of the area.

The Palo de Mayo
May brings an outpouring of joy, dance, and music in Bluefields on Nicaragua's Caribbean Coast. Residents and visitors dance to reggae music around the Palo de Mayo (May Pole), and every night is a celebration with feasting, parades, and costumes.

Volcano Climbing
The challenge of climbing one of Nicaragua's perfectly cone-shaped volcanoes is irresistible for many hikers. Some of the hikes, for example the three-hour climb to the lip of Volcán Cosiguina, can be difficult. However, daring climbers are rewarded with spectacular views.

Managua
Managua's two cathedrals are a study in contrast, one symbolizing the past and the other hope for the future. The historic Catedral Santiago de los Caballeros stands in dignified ruins, irreparably damaged by the 1972 earthquake, while the new Catedral de la Inmaculada Concepción de María showcases modern architecture.

Colonial City
Granada was founded in 1523 by the Spaniards. The Antiguo Convento San Francisco, built by Franciscan monks in 1529, is one of the main attractions. It now houses both a beautiful church and an extensive museum, displaying, among other things, thirty pre-Columbian stone carvings that were found on a nearby island.

Primativist Paintings
Solentiname Island, on the southern tip of Lake Nicaragua, is famous for its world-renowned, colorful art filled with strong patterns. The tradition of painting started in 1966, when a priest encouraged local jícaro cup carvers (who decorated drinking cups made from a gourd-like plant) to put their pictures on canvas.

ABOUT THE CULTURE

OFFICIAL NAME
Republic of Nicaragua

DESCRIPTION OF NATIONAL FLAG
Three equal horizontal bands of blue, white, and blue, with the national coat of arms in the center: a triangle encircled by the words Republica de Nicaragua and America Central.

NATIONAL ANTHEM
"Salve a tí, Nicaragua" ("Hail to thee, Nicaragua") was officially adopted on August 25, 1971. Salomon Ibarra Mayorga wrote the lyrics and Luis A. Delgadillo arranged the music.

CAPITAL
Managua

PROVINCES AND TERRITORIES
Fifteen departments: Boaco, Carazo, Chinandega, Chontales, Estelí, Granada, Jinotega, León, Madriz, Managua, Masaya, Matagalpa, Nueva Segovia, Río San Juan, Rivas. Two autonomous regions: Atlantico Norte and Atlantico Sur.

OTHER MAJOR CITIES
León, Chinandega, Granada, Masaya, Matagalpa, Estelí, and Jinotepe.

POPULATION
5,907,881 (2015)

ETHNIC GROUPS
Mestizo 69 percent, white 17 percent, black 9 percent, Amerindian 5 percent

RELIGION
Roman Catholic 58.5 percent, Protestant 23.2 percent, none 15.7 percent (2014)

LANGUAGES
Spanish (official), English, and indigenous languages on Caribbean Coast

LITERACY RATE
82.8 percent (2015)

IMPORTANT HOLIDAYS AND ANNIVERSARIES
Easter (March/April), Independence Day (September 15), Purísma (December 7), Christmas (December 25)

LEADERS IN POLITICS
President José Daniel Ortega Saavedra (since January 2007)
Vice President Moises Omar Halleslevens Acevedo (since January 2012)

ELECTIONS
President and vice president are elected on the same ticket by popular vote for a five-year term

TIMELINE

IN NICARAGUA	IN THE WORLD

10,000 BCE
Footprints made by humans as they carry heavy objects in Acahualinca.

6,000 BCE
First known inhabitants of Nicaragua's Caribbean coast leave shell deposits.

753 BCE
Rome is founded.

116–117 CE
The peak of the Roman Empire under Emperor Trajan (98–117 CE)

500 CE
Pre-Columbian people carve stone monuments on Zapatera Island in Lake Nicaragua.

600 CE
Height of Mayan civilization

800–1200
More pre-Columbian peoples move to the shores of Lake Nicaragua.

1000
The Chinese perfect gunpowder and begin to use it in warfare.

1502
Christopher Columbus sails along Nicaragua's eastern coast.

1524
Francisco Hernández de Córdoba starts the first Spanish settlement in Nicaragua.

1530
Beginning of transatlantic slave trade organized by the Portuguese in Africa.

1544
Nicaragua comes under the administration of the audencia of Guatemala.

1558–1603
Reign of Elizabeth I of England

1620
Pilgrims sail the *Mayflower* to America.

1740
Mosquito Coast becomes a British dependency.

1776
US Declaration of Independence

1789–1799
The French Revolution

1821
Nicaragua declares independence from Spanish rule.

1838
Nicaragua becomes a sovereign nation.

1856
US adventurer William Walker proclaims himself president of Nicaragua.

1861
The US Civil War begins.

1869
The Suez Canal is opened.

1911
The United States gains control over Nicaragua's finances.

1914
World War I begins.

IN NICARAGUA	IN THE WORLD

1937
Anastasio Somoza García becomes president of Nicaragua.

1939
World War II begins.

1945
World War II ends

1949
The North Atlantic Treaty Organization (NATO) is formed.

1956
Somoza is assassinated by poet Rigoberto López Pérez.

1957
The Russians launch *Sputnik*.

1966–1969
The Chinese Cultural Revolution

1967
Anastasio Somoza Debayle becomes president.

1972
A major earthquake destroys Managua.

1980
The FSLN wins control of the government. Contra War begins.

1986
Nuclear power disaster at Chernobyl in Ukraine

1990
Violeta de Barrios Chamorro becomes Nicaragua's first woman president.

1991
Breakup of the Soviet Union

1997
Arnoldo Alemán wins presidential election.

1997
Hong Kong is returned to China.

1998
Hurricane Mitch devastates Nicaragua.

2001
Enrique Bolaños becomes president.

2001
Terrorists crash planes in New York, Washington, DC, and Pennsylvania.

2003
Former president Alemán jailed for corruption.

2003
War in Iraq

2007
Daniel Ortega elected president.

2008
The United States elects its first black president, Barack Obama

2011
Ortega wins second consecutive term.

2015
Work begins on Nicaragua canal project.

2015
NASA's *New Horizons* spacecraft flies by Pluto.

GLOSSARY

barrio
A poor neighborhood.

brigadistas
Volunteers in the Literacy Crusade.

campesinos
Peasant farmers.

compadrazgo **(kahm-pah-DRAHZ-goh)**
Godparents, chosen by a child's parents to assist, among other things, in the child's moral upbringing.

conquistadores
Spanish conquerors who went to Central America in the sixteenth century.

Contra
A counter-revolutionary, someone who opposes the Sandinistas.

dictator
A ruler who assumes absolute authority.

fictive kin
People who are not relatives but are so close that they consider each other family.

filibuster
A person engaging in unauthorized warfare against a foreign country.

fritanga **(free-TAN-ga)**
An outdoor stand that sells grilled meats and other foods.

gallo pinto **(GUY-oh PEEHN-toh)**
A favorite dish made with white rice, red beans, and spices; the name means "painted rooster" because of the red and white colors.

guerrilla
Covert military fighter opposed to the government; or the clandestine tactics used by such a fighter.

junta
A group of people who controls the government after a revolution or coup d'état.

machismo
Strong, aggressive male pride or behavior.

mestizo
Someone who has both Indian and Spanish ancestry.

nacatamale **(nah-caw-ta-MAL-eh)**
One of Nicaragua's traditional foods; a cornmeal tamale filled with pork, rice, potato, onion, tomato, and green pepper.

refresco **(ray-FREHS-koh)**
A cool fruit drink served in a plastic bag.

remittance
A sum of money sent to a person or place; or the sending of money in payment for a transaction.

Sandinista
Follower of General Augusto César Sandino, or a member of the FSLN.

FOR FURTHER INFORMATION

BOOKS

Belli, Gioconda. *The Country Under My Skin: A Memoir of Love and War*. New York: Alfred A. Knopf, 2002.

Cardenal, Fernando. *Faith and Joy: Memoirs of a Priest Revolutionary*. Maryknoll, NY: Orbis Books, 2015.

Kinzer, Stephen. *Blood of Brothers: Life and War in Nicaragua*. Cambridge, MA: Harvard University Press, 2007.

WEBSITES

CIA World Factbook, Nicaragua
www.cia.gov/library/publications/the-world-factbook/geos/nu.html

The Culture Trip, theculturetrip.com/central-america/nicaragua

Lonely Planet, www.lonelyplanet.com/nicaragua

Nicaragua.com. www.nicaragua.com

Nicaragua Dispatch, nicaraguadispatch.com

Vianica.com, vianica.com

FILMS

Carla's Song, Fox Lorber, 1999 DVD

The Mosquito Coast, Warner Home Video, 2008

Nicaragua No Parasan, Frontline Films, 2008

MUSIC

Antologia, Dúo Guardabarranco (Katia and Salvador Cardenal), Guardabarranco, 2005

Soy Juventud, Dúo Guardabarranco, Moka Discos, 2009

Marimba: Music from Nicaragua, International Music, 2000

Nicaragua Presente! Music From Nicaragua Libre, Rounder Select, 1992

BIBLIOGRAPHY

Associated Press. "Rosario Murillo: Nicaragua's 'First Comrade'" *The New York Times*,
   July 28, 2014
   www.nytimes.com/aponline/2014/07/28/world/americas/ap-lt-nicaragua-rosario-murillo.html

BBC News Country Profile, Nicaragua Timeline. news.bbc.co.uk/2/hi/americas/country_
   profiles/1225283.stm

BBC News, Profile: Nicaraguan President Daniel Ortega.
   www.bbc.com/news/world-latin-america-15544315

CIA World Factbook, Nicaragua
   www.cia.gov/library/publications/the-world-factbook/geos/nu.html

Hutt, David. "Is Nicaragua's education system failing?" *The Tico Times*, Jan. 31, 2013
   www.ticotimes.net/2013/02/01/is-nicaragua-s-education-system-failing

Johnson, Tim. "Deja vu in Nicaragua? President Ortega and first lady wield 'dynastic' power." *The
   Christian Science Monitor*, Jan. 10, 2014. www.csmonitor.com/World/Americas/2014/0110/
   Deja-vu-in-Nicaragua-President-Ortega-and-first-lady-wield-dynastic-power

Miller, Greg. "Why the Plan to Dig a Canal Across Nicaragua Could Be a Very Bad Idea." *Wired*,
   Feb. 26, 2014. www.wired.com/2014/02/nicaragua-canal

Nicaragua.com. www.nicaragua.com

Nicaragua Community www.nicaragua-community.com

Nicaragua Dispatch, nicaraguadispatch.com

Rogers, Tim, "Is That a Rooster in Your Mouth?" *Time*, Feb. 16, 2007 content.time.com/time/
   world/article/0,8599,1590985,00.html

Serrano, Alfonso. "Titanic Canal Project Divides Nicaragua." Al Jazeera America, April 6, 2015
   projects.aljazeera.com/2015/04/nicaragua-canal

UNICEF, www.unicef.org/infobycountry/nicaragua_statistics.html

Vianica.com, vianica.com

World Bank, Central America. www.worldbank.org/en/country/centralamerica

INDEX

INDEX